The War of Creation

富育光 著　刘艳杰 译

辽宁民族出版社

图书在版编目（CIP）数据

天宫大战 = The War of Creation : 汉、英 / 富育光著 ; 刘艳杰译. -- 沈阳 : 辽宁民族出版社, 2021.11
ISBN 978-7-5497-2469-7

Ⅰ. ①天… Ⅱ. ①富… ②刘… Ⅲ. ①满族－民间故事－作品集－中国－汉、英 Ⅳ. ①I277.3

中国版本图书馆CIP数据核字(2021)第186204号

天宫大战　The War of Creation
TIANGONG DAZHAN

出版发行者：辽宁民族出版社
地　　　址：沈阳市和平区十一纬路25号　邮编：110003
印　刷　者：辽宁鼎籍数码科技有限公司
幅 面 尺 寸：170mm × 240mm
印　　　张：11.25
字　　　数：110千字
出 版 时 间：2021年11月第1版
印 刷 时 间：2021年11月第1次印刷
责 任 编 辑：王　智
助 理 编 辑：杜璐珊
封 面 设 计：杜　江
责 任 校 对：王　荷

标 准 书 号：ISBN 978-7-5497-2469-7
定　　　价：58.00元

网址：www.lnmzcbs.com　　邮购热线：024-23284335
淘宝网店：http://lnmz2013.taobao.com
如有印装质量问题，请与出版社联系调换　　联系电话：024-23284340

序言

今天，我非常高兴，非常兴奋，因为由大连民族大学英语教师刘艳杰所翻译的《天宫大战》即将正式出版，并邀请我为该书做序言。这是继《乌布西奔妈妈研究》和《西林安班玛发》英语版出版之后，问世的又一部由大连民族大学英语教师翻译的英语版满族史诗。

满族是我国具有悠久历史的古老民族之一，在漫长的社会历史长河中创造、发展并继承了灿烂多彩的民族文化。流传在满族一些群众中脍炙人口的说部艺术，便是其中一个典型代表，并被列入第一批国家级非物质文化遗产名录。满族说部，俗称“讲古”，满语称为“乌勒本（ulabun）”，意为家族传承的故事，即流传于满族各大家族内部，讲述本民族，特别是本宗族历史上曾经发生的故事。满族说部遗存主要有“窝车库乌勒本”“包衣乌勒本”和“巴图鲁乌勒本”三个方面的内容。其中，窝车库乌勒本由满族各部落、各姓氏历代萨满讲述并世代传承，以萨满教神话与历代萨满的故事为主要内容，俗称“神龛上的故事”。《天宫大战》是窝车库乌勒本的典型代表。

《天宫大战》讲述了创世之初，善与恶、光明与黑暗、存在与死亡两种势力的激烈抗衡，是萨满教的创世神话。谈到创世神话，很多西方学者都认为中国没有系统的创世神话，而我要说，《天宫大战》讲述的神话反映的是我国旧石器时代母系氏族社会的满族先人历史，它比古希腊神话《伊利亚特》《奥德赛》早一个时代。而且，《天宫大战》中反映了人类在艰苦的生存竞争中产生并积蓄的开拓精神。正是这种勇武不屈的生存意识和观念成为了北方诸民族不畏各种自然力量的精神营养，堪称民族文化的精萃和古卉，对满族社会、历史、文化的研究，乃至中国北方民族的社会学、民俗学、文艺学及宗教学的深入研究，都大有裨益。

在入主中原以前，满族几乎没有以文本形式记录本民族历史的习惯，当时人们记录历史最常见的方式，就是通过部落酋长或萨满来口传历史、教育子孙。有谚曰："老的不讲古，小的失了谱。"讲古，就是利用大家最为喜闻乐见的说书形式，去追念祖先、教育后人，借此增强民族或宗族的凝聚力。我所讲述的满族神话《天宫大战》出自本家族传承下来的古老神词。我的父亲富希陆在20世纪30年代曾为小学老师，他自幼热衷于本民族文化，通晓满文，精通古文，且长期生活在满族聚居区。在那个年代，满族先民的原始文化还有大量遗存。我的父亲曾听一位住在黑龙江省孙吴县名为白蒙古的大萨满唱过《天宫大战》，然后他用满文进行了整理，并传给了我。《天宫大战》经历了数次劫难，父亲和我凭着对民族文化的珍爱和对自己祖先的深厚感情，保存下这一珍贵的人类文化遗产。

我国对满族说部的收集整理工作主要是从1981年开始的，吉林省社会科学工作者奔赴吉林、黑龙江、辽宁、北京、河北、四川等满族聚居地区进行调查，寻访满族说部传承人，了解说部在各地的流传情况，并对一些传承人讲述的说部进行了录音。到了20世纪90年代，为了将《天宫大战》等满族神话的满文和原始图画文字翻译成汉语，我遍访为数不多的北方少数民族萨满，破译了部分原始图画文字，将主要的内容整理成书，并于1990年由辽宁大学出版社出版。2006年5月，满族说部被国务院列入第一批国家级非物质文化遗产名录。

满族说部最初是用满语口头传承，后来随着满汉文化不断交流融合，说部的形式不断变化，目前主要以汉语作为传承语言，其文本也主要是汉文。真正意义上的满族说部翻译传播及研究是在说部"文本化"

之后以翻译（语内翻译和语际翻译）的方式进行的。国内对满族说部的翻译首先是由满文译为汉文；而翻译成外文（如英译）的实践和理论研究才小荷初露，发展空间巨大。目前，《天宫大战》的部分内容相继被翻译成德、日、韩文出版，但是《天宫大战》的完整英译本仍为空白。将其译为世界通用语言——英语，让海内外读者了解和研究这部满族创世神话，对发掘中国少数民族文化典籍的整体文化价值、推动少数民族文化传承、增进我国各民族之间以及中外文化之间的交流有着重要的现实意义。

正是满族说部和满族文化让我与大连民族大学结缘，与大连民族大学的英语教师们结缘。大连民族大学有着一批为满族文化的研究和对外传播勤奋工作的学者和教师。他们给我留下了深刻的印象，我十分感谢他们。据我了解，以王维波教授为代表的东北少数民族典籍翻译团队，自 2010 年始做了大量东北少数民族史诗的英文翻译与研究工作。满族说部则是其中之一。

《天宫大战》的英译是中国少数民族文学翻译理论和翻译方法研究的实例，这就要求译者不但要有扎实的语言功底、得当的翻译方法和策略，还要有对源文本及满族传统文化有着深入的理解和领悟。这对翻译其他少数民族文学作品也可以提供一定的借鉴。

最后，我衷心希望大连民族大学的学者和教师继续发挥地缘优势，立足东北，服务民族，以《天宫大战》英译本的出版为发端，再接再厉，为传播中华民族传统文化作出更多的贡献。

富育光

2019 年 7 月 31 日

Preface

Today, I am very happy, very excited, because the War of Creation, translated by Liu Yanjie, an English teacher at Dalian Minzu University, will be officially published, and I have the honor of being invited to do the preface for the book. This is another English version of the Manchu epic translated by the English teachers of Dalian Minzu University, following the publication of the English version of "A Study of The Mother of Wubushiben" and "Xilinanban mafa".

Manchu nationality is one of the ancient nationalities with a long history in China. It has created, developed and inherited the splendid national culture and art in the long social history. The art of literary story-telling, which is popular among some people of Manchu, is the most representative national cultural heritage. The Manchu Story-telling Series, commonly known as "telling ancient stories" and "Ulabun" in Manchu, means the stories passed down from family to family, that is, the stories passed down in the Manchu families, telling the stories that happened in the history of the nation, especially the clan. The remains of The Manchu story-telling series are mainly preserved in three aspects: "Wocheku Ulabun", "Baoyi Ulabun" and "Batulu Ulabun". Among them, Wocheku Ulabun is narrated and passed down from generation to generation by Shamans of various tribes, with Shamanistic myths and stories of Shamans as the main content, commonly known as "the story on the shrine". "The War of Creation" is a typical representative of Wocheku Ulabun.

The War of Creation, a shamanistic creation myth, tells the fierce confrontation between good and evil, light and darkness, existence and death at the beginning of creation. When it comes to the creation myth, western scholars all believe that there is no systematic creation myth in China. However, I would like to say that the myth told in "The War of Creation" reflects the history of Manchu ancestors of matriarchal society in the Paleolithic Age of China, which is a historical era earlier than the ancient Greek myth "the Iliad and the Odyssey". Moreover, "The War of Creation" reflects the pioneering spirit generated and accumulated by human beings in the arduous struggle for survival. It was this brave and noble survival consciousness and the concept that has become the northern minorities' spiritual nourishment for defying all kinds of natural forces, which is one of the quintessence of national culture in China. Meanwhile, it helps the study of Manchu society, history, culture, and even the in-depth study of sociology, folklore, literature and religion of the northern minorities in China.

Before entering the Central Plains of China, the Manchu had almost no habit of recording their national history in the form of text. At that time, the most common way for people to record their history was to teach their descendants with oral history through tribal chiefs or Shamans. There is a saying: "The old do not tell the past, the young lost their pedigree." To tell ancient stories is to use the most popular form of story-telling to remember ancestors and educate descendants so as to strengthen the cohesion of a nation or clan. The Manchu myth "The War of Creation" originally came from the ancient sacred words of our family. My father Fu Xilu was a primary school teacher in the 1930s. He was keen on his own ethnic culture since childhood. He was proficient in Manchu and ancient philology and lived in ethnic minority areas for a long time. At that time, there were still many relics of the primitive culture of the Manchu ancestors. My father listened to the story of The War of Creation sung by a great shaman named Bai Mongol in Sunwu County, Heilongjiang Province. He compiled it in Manchu and sent it to me. "The War of Creation" has survived several disasters. My father and I have preserved this particularly precious cultural heritage of mankind with our love for culture and our deep affection for our ancestors.

The collection and sorting work of Manchu story-telling series in China mainly started in 1981, when social workers went to Jilin, Heilongjiang, Liaoning, Beijing, Hebei, Sichuan Manchu populated areas for investigation, searching for Manchu story-telling inheritors, finding out its spreading situation around China, and recording some of the Manchu stories told by inheritors. In the 1990s, in order to translate Manchu myths such as The War of Creation into Chinese, I visited a small number of Shamans in northern China, deciphered some of the original characters, and compiled the main contents into a book, which was published by Liaoning University Press in 1990. In May 2006, the Manchu Storytelling Series was approved by The State Council as the first batch of national intangible cultural heritage.

At first, Manchu story-telling was passed down orally in Manchu language. Later, with the continuous exchange and integration of Manchu and Han cultures, the form of story-telling kept changing. At present,

Chinese is mainly used as the language of inheritance and its text is also mainly in Chinese. In the real sense, the study of translation and transmission of Manchu story-telling is carried out through translation (intralingual translation and interlingual translation) after the "textualization" of story-telling. The translation of Manchu story-telling in China is first from Manchu to Chinese. However, the practical and theoretical research of translation into foreign languages (such as English translation) has just begun to show its great potential for development. At present, part of The War of Creation has been translated into German, Japanese and Korean, but its complete English translation remains blank. To translate it into English, the universal language of the world, so that readers at home and abroad can understand and study this creation myth of Manchu, is of great practical significance to explore the overall cultural value of Chinese minority cultural classics, promote the cultural inheritance of minority nationalities, and enhance the communication between various ethnic groups in China and between Chinese and foreign cultures.

It was the Manchu storytelling Series and Manchu culture that brought me to Dalian Minzu University and the English teachers there. Dalian Minzu University has a group of scholars and teachers who work hard for the study and dissemination of Manchu culture. They made an unforgettable good impression on me and I am much appreciated. As far as I know, the northeast minority classics translation team, represented by Professor Wang Weibo, has been doing a lot of English translation and research work of northeast minority epics since 2010. Manchu Story-telling Series is one of them.

The English translation of The War of Creation is a case study of the translation theories and methods of Chinese minority literature. For the translator, it is necessary not only to have a solid language foundation, proper translation methods and strategies, but also to have a deep understanding of the source text and traditional Manchu culture. The works can also provide some reference for the translation of other minority literature works.

Finally, I sincerely hope that the scholars and teachers of Dalian Minzu University will continue to give full play to their geographical advantages, base themselves on northeast China and serve the nation. Starting with the publication of the English version of The War of Creation, they will continue their efforts and make more contributions to the spread of traditional Chinese culture.

Fu Yuguang

July 31, 2019

目 录

Contents

引子

黑龙江四季屯满族白蒙古老人讲窝车库乌勒本[1]，
犹如东方的太阳神光，
照彻大地。
博额德音姆安班[2]萨满那，
现在，
所有的供果都摆上了祭坛，
千网得来的安班阿斤[3]，
已经贡献上了。
这是你的海中坐骑，
我们是从 1000 多千米的东海给你网来的。
还有成百上千只山雀，
美丽的红顶鹤，
都是你的使者。
它们听从你神鼓的声响，
一起鸣唱，
鸣唱明天，
明天美好的日子。

---

1 窝车库乌勒本：满语，意为神龛上的故事。
2 安班：满语，意为大。
3 安班阿斤：满语，意为大鳇鱼。

Prelude

Bai Mongolia, an elderly Manchu man from Siji Village of Heilongjiang Province, tells the creation epic of Wochekuwuleben[1]*:*

Like the sacred sunlight in the east,
You enlighten the earth all over.
Boedeyinmu!
My Anban[2] Shaman!
At the moment,
All fruit offerings,
Have been set on the altar,
A hard-caught Anban'ajin[3]
Has been consecrated as well.
It is your sea mount,
Caught with net
From the East Sea over two miles away.
Still, hundreds even thousands of titmice,
And beautiful red crown cranes,
Are all your messengers.
Following the beat of your holy drum,
They are singing all together,
Singing of tomorrow:
A bright new day.

---

1 Wocheku wuleben:Manchu language, the story at the shrine.
2 Anban: Manchu language, chief or big.
3 Anban'ajin: Manchu language, big beluga.

头腓凌[1]

从萨哈连[2]下游的东方，

走来骑九叉神鹿的博额德音姆萨满，

天上彩霞闪光的时候，

萨哈连水跳着浪花的时候，

天上刮下来金翅鲤鱼，

树窟里爬出来四腿的银蛇。

不知是几辈奶奶管家的年头，

从萨哈连下游的东方，

走来了骑着九叉神鹿的博额德音姆萨满，

百余岁了，

还红颜满面，

白发满头，

还年富力强。

是神鹰给她的精力，

是鱼神给她的水性，

是阿布卡赫赫[3]给她的神寿，

是百鸟给她的歌喉，

1 “腓凌”：满语，回或次序之意。

2 萨哈连：满语，意为黑龙江。

3 阿布卡赫赫：满族创世神话中的女性始祖，天神。

是百兽给她的坐骑。

百枝除邪，

百事通神，

百难卜知，

恰拉器[1]传谕着神示。

厚爱情深呵，

犹如东方的太阳神光

照彻大地……

1　恰拉器：萨满祭祀时使用的扎板，可拍击出节奏作为伴奏。

Chapter I[1]

From the east of the lower reaches of Sahalian[2] ,
Came a sacred deer with nine antlers,
On which sat the Shaman Boedeyinmu.
When the rosy clouds were shining in the sky,
When the waves were dancing on the Sahalian River,
Gold-fin carps were blown down from the sky,
Four-legged silver snakes crawled out of the tree cave.
The year no one knew which generation of grandma kept house,
From the east of the lower reaches of Sahalian,
Came a sacred deer with nine antlers,
On which sat the Shaman Boedeyinmu.
Though over one hundred years old,
She was still in ruddy health;
Though wearing white hair on head,
She still looked young and vigorous.
The sacred eagle granted her the mighty energy,
The sacred fish offered her the swimming skill,
Abukahehe[3] gave her immortal longevity,
Hundreds of birds granted her beautiful voice,

---

1 Chapter:In Manchu language,Feiling（腓凌） is the equivalent of chapter.
2 Sahalian: Manchu language, Heilongjiang River.
3 Abukahehe: Renowned as the first goddess in the Manchu Creation Myth.

Hundreds of beasts offered her the sturdy horse.

With hundreds of branches,

She drove away the evil;

Through communicating with the gods,

She knew all fortune;

By practicing divination,

She predicted all calamities.

Qialaqi[1] spoke out the oracle.

Like the sacred sunlight in the east,

Her deep love and affection,

Enlightened the earth all over……

1 Qialaqi: A musical instrument used in shaman sacrificial rituals to beat out the tune as accompaniment.

贰腓凌

世上最先有的是什么?

最古老的时候是什么样?

世上最古老的时候,

是不分天、不分地的水泡泡。

天像水,

水像天,

天水相连,

像水一样流溢不定。

水泡渐渐长,

水泡渐渐多,

水泡里生出阿布卡赫赫 。

起初她像水泡那么小,

可她越长越大。

有水的地方、

有水泡的地方,

都有阿布卡赫赫。

她小小的,像水珠,

她长长的,高过寰宇,

她大得变成天穹。

她身轻能浮于空宇,

她身重能沉入水底。

她无处不在,

无处不有，

无处不生。

她的体魄谁也看不清，

只有在小水珠里，

才能看清她是七彩神光，

白蓝白亮，

湛湛。

她能气生万物，

光生万物，

身生万物。

空宇中万物愈多，

便分出清浊，

清清上升，

浊浊下降，

光亮上升，

雾气下降，

上清下浊。

于是，

阿布卡赫赫下身

又裂生出巴那姆赫赫[1]。

这样，

清光成天，

浊雾成地，

1 巴那姆赫赫：满族创世神话中的地神。

才有了天地姊妹尊神。
清清为气，
白光为亮，
气浮于天，
光游于光，
气静光燥，
气止光行，
气光相搏，
气光骤离，
气不束光。
于是，
阿布卡赫赫上身
裂生出卧勒多赫赫[1]，
好动不止，
周行天地，
司掌明亮。
阿布卡赫赫、
巴那姆赫赫、
卧勒多赫赫，
同身同根，
同现同显，
同存同在，

1　卧勒多赫赫：也称希里女神。相传，她背着皮褡裢带，每当夜晚来临，便往天上撒满星斗，故为布星女神。

同生同孕。

阿布卡气生云雷，

巴那姆肤生谷泉，

卧勒多用阿布卡赫赫的眼睛

布生顺、毕牙、那丹那拉呼[1]，

三神永生永育，

育有大千。

1 顺、毕牙、那丹那拉呼：满语，意为日、月、小北斗星。

Chapter II

What came first into the world?

What did the world look like at the very beginning?

The world at the very beginning,

Was a bubble of water,

With no distinction between the heaven and the earth.

Heaven looked like water,

Water looked like heaven;

Heaven was tightly connected with water,

And ceaselessly flowed like water.

Water bubble grew and grew,

Water bubble multiplied and multiplied,

And in the water bubble,

Abukahehe was miraculously born.

At first she was as tiny as a bubble,

Then she grew larger and larger.

Where there was water,

Where there is a bubble,

There was Abukahehe.

Tiny as a bubble,

Yet higher than the welkin,

She finally grew as great as sky.

So light that she could float in the air,

So heavy that she could sink to the water bottom.
She existed everywhere,
Went everywhere,
And reproduced everywhere.
No one could see her figure;
Only in the tiny bubble,
Could one see her sacred seven-color light,
White, blue and bright,
In brilliance.
With air she created myriads of creatures;
With light she created myriads of creatures;
With her own body she created myriads of creatures.
As more creatures are floating in the air,
The clear separated from the muddy;
The clear ascended,
While the muddy descended;
The light rose,
While the fog fell;
Consequently the clear was on the top,
While the muddy was at the bottom.
Then,
Abukahehe's lower part
Split up into Banamuhehe[1].
The clear light turned into the heaven,
The muddy fog turned into the earth,

1 Banamuhehe: The goddess of the earth in creation myth of Manchu.

And thereby established
The Sister Goddesses of Heaven and Earth.
So clear the air was,
So bright the light was;
The air was floating around the sky,
The light was flowing among the light;
The air was quiet while the light was restless,
The air stood still while the light traveled around;
Tightly the air tangled with the light,
Abruptly the air separated with the light,
Hardly could the air fetter the light.
Subsequently,
Abukahehe's upper body
Split into Woleduohehe [1],
Who was active and restless,
Traveled between the heaven and the earth,
And governed the light.
Abukahehe,
Banamuhehe,
And Woleduohehe,
Shared the same holy body,
Appeared and showed up together,
Lived and existed together,
Conceived and reproduced offspring together.
With expiration Abuka made clouds and thunder,

1 Woleduohehe: Also called Goddess Xili. According to the legend, she carried a birch-bark bag on the back, and scattered stars over the sky at night, thus is also called the goddess of the stars.

With skin Banamu made valley spring;

With Abuka's eyes Woleduo made

Shun, Beya and Nadannalahu [1].

Three goddesses lived and reproduced perpetually,

So came out all creatures in the universe.

1 Shun, Beya and Nadannalahu: Manchu language, refer to the Sun, the Moon and the Little Dipper.

叁腓凌

世上怎么有了男人、女人，
有了虫兽，
有了禀赋呢？
阿布卡赫赫性慈，
巴那姆赫赫性好酣，
卧勒多赫赫性烈。
原来三神生物相约合力，
巴那姆赫赫嗜睡不醒，
阿布卡赫赫和卧勒多赫赫两神造人。
最先生出来的全是女人，
所以，
女人心慈性烈。
等巴那姆赫赫醒来想起造人事，
姐妹已走，
情急催生，
因无光而生，
生出了天禽、地兽、土虫，
都是白天喜睡，
夜出活动。
因无阿布卡赫赫的善良天性，
它们相残相食，
暴殄肆虐，

还有虫类小兽惧光怕亮，
癖好穴行。

那么又怎么有了男人呢？
阿布卡赫赫见世上只生有女人，
就从身上揪下块肉，
做出个敖钦女神，
生有九个头，
这样就可以有的头睡觉，
有的头保持清醒。
阿布卡赫赫还从卧勒多女神身上要了块肉，
给她做了八只手臂，
有的手累了歇息，
有的手不累可以劳作。
让她侍守在巴那姆赫赫身旁，
使巴那姆赫赫总被推摇，
酣不成眠。
阿布卡赫赫、卧勒多赫赫
这回同巴那姆赫赫一起造男人。
巴那姆赫赫身边
有捣乱的敖钦女神，
不得酣睡，
姐妹在一旁催促她快造男人，
她忙三迭四不耐烦地

顺手抓下一把肩胛骨和腋毛，
和姐妹的慈肉、烈肉一起
揉成了一个男人。
所以，
男人性烈心慈，
还比女人身强力壮，
因其是骨头做的。
不过是肩骨和腋毛合成的，
所以，
男人身上的须发髯毛比女人多。
巴那姆赫赫躺卧时，
把肩胛骨压在身下，
肩胛骨就有了泥，
所以，
男人比女人浊泥多，
心术比女人叵测。
阿布卡赫赫说：
男人和女人哪里不同啊？
卧勒多赫赫也不知男人什么样，
巴那姆赫赫便想到
学着天禽、地兽、土虫的模样造男人。
男人多一个“索索”[1]，
她抓下身上一块肉，

1 索索：满语，意为男性生殖器。

闭着眼睛，
一下子安在山鸡乌勒胡玛身上。
所以，
山鸡屁股上
多个鸡尖和一个小肉桩。
姐妹说安错了，
她又抓下一块肉，
安在水鸭肚子底下，
所以，
水鸭类动物的“索索”，
都长在肚腔里。
姐妹又埋怨安错了，
她便抓下一块细骨棒
安到了身边母鹿的肚子底下，
母鹿变成了公鹿。
从此凡是獐鹿狍犴类动物，
雄性的“索索”像利针，
锋利无比，
常在发情时刺毙母鹿。
姐妹俩又生气地说给安措了，
巴那姆赫赫这时才苏醒过来，
慌慌忙忙从身边的野熊胯下要了个“索索”，
安在了她们合做成的男人形体的胯下。
所以，

男人的“索索”，

跟熊罴的“索索”

长短模样相似，

是跟熊身上借来的。

所以，

兽族百禽比人早来到世上。

Chapter III

How did the men and women come into the world?
How did the worms and animals come into the world?
How did they have their natural endowment?
By nature,
Abukahehe was kind,
Banamuhehe was somnolent,
Woleduohehe was hot-tempered.
Three goddesses had previously agreed
To cooperate in creating mankind;
But Banamuhehe was in sound sleep day and night,
So Abukahehe and Woleduohehe
Had to create humans on their own.
At first,
All humans they created were women;
Therefore,
Women were kind-hearted yet hot-tempered.
When Banamuhehe woke up
And remembered the work of creation,
Her sisters had gone away.
In such an anxiety,
She hastened to fulfill her work;
Since created in the dark,

The birds, the beasts and the worms
All tended to sleep in the day,
But came out at night.
Without Abukahehe's kind soul,
They killed and ate each other,
Committed violence and wreaked havoc;
In addition,
Worms and small animals were afraid of light,
But fond of living underground.

Then how did the men come into the world?
Seeing there were only women living in the world,
Abukahehe picked a piece of flesh off her body,
And created the goddess Aoqin,
Who had nine heads,
So when some of her heads slept,
Others could still stay awake.
Besides,
Abukahehe asked from Woleduohehe
For some flesh to make eight arms for Aoqin,
So some of her hands could
Have a rest when they were tired,
While others could still keep working hard.
Since Aoqin was ordered to attend to Banamuhehe,

Banamuhehe was pushed and shaken without cease,
Unable to fall asleep though sleepy.
Finally Abukahehe and Woleduohehe
Could create men together with Banamuhehe.
With Aoqin rustling around,
Banamuhehe could not fall into sound sleep;
With two sisters urging her to create men,
She, in haste and impatience,
Picked off her shoulder bones and armpit hairs,
Mixed them with her sisters'
Kind-hearted and hot-tempered flesh,
And kneaded them into a man.
Therefore,
Men were hot-tempered yet kind-hearted,
And physically stronger than women,
For they were made from bones.
But because the bones was mixed of
Shoulder bones and armpit hairs,
Men had much more hair than women.
Banamuhehe tended to lie down,
With her shoulder bones under the body,
Which stained with mud;
Therefore,
Men were much dirtier than women,

And hatched much more evil intentions than women.

Abukahehe asked,

"What differs men from women on earth?"

Actually,

Woleduohehe had no idea at all

About what the men should be like.

Suddenly,

A good idea hit upon Banamuhehe

That they could create men's body

In the similar way they created

the birds, the animals, and the worms.

Considering Men should have a "suosuo" [1],

She, with her eyes closed,

Picked a piece of flesh off her body,

Pressed it onto the pheasant's body without thinking;

Therefore,

On the pheasant's butt,

There is a rump and a little flesh organ.

Two sisters blamed her for the mistake;

Then she picked another piece of flesh off her body,

Pressed it onto the belly of a water duck;

Therefore,

The water ducks' suosuo,

1 Suosuo: Manchu language, penis.

All grow in their belly.

Again, two sisters blamed her for the mistake;

Then she picked a small bone off her body,

Pressed it under onto a doe's belly beside her,

Who subsequently turned into a stag;

Since then,

In all deer species,

Male stags had a suosuo as sharp as a needle,

Which was keen-edged in the extreme,

And often stabbed doe to death in full rut.

Once Again,

Two sisters were angry with her mistake.

Now totally awake,

Banamuhehe hastily picked a 'suosuo'

Off a wild bear's crotch nearby,

Pressed it onto the crotch of the man

That they created together;

Therefore,

Men's suosuo resembled bears' suosuo

In shape and length,

For it was originally taken from a bear.

Hence,

Birds and animals came into the world,

Earlier than mankind.

肆腓凌

世上最早的恶魔怎么诞生的？

最凶的魔鬼是谁？

敖钦女神的九个头颅，

想着的事超过百禽百兽，

眼睛时时有看着之物，

耳朵时时有听着之声，

鼻子时时有闻着之味，

嘴里时时有吃着之食。

所以，

她把百禽百兽的智慧和能耐都学通了，

她的手时时推摇着巴那姆赫赫，

练得力可撼山岳，

猛劲无穷。

她总看守着巴那姆赫赫，

也甚觉没趣，

有时就发怒吼闹。

因她的身子来自阿布卡赫赫和卧勒多赫赫

吐出的云气和烈火，

更会打破巴那姆赫赫的宁静。

巴那姆赫赫本来就

烦恶敖钦女神，

一气之下用身上的

两大块山砬子打过去，
一块山尖变成了
敖钦女神头上的一只角，
直插天穹；
另一块山尖压在敖钦女神肚下，
变成了“索索”。
敖钦女神被两块山尖一打，
马上变了神形，
成为一角九头八臂的两性怪神。
她自己有“索索”，
能自生自育，
又有阿布卡赫赫、卧勒多赫赫、巴那姆赫赫
身上的骨肉魂魄，
又有九头学到的百能百技，
有利角可刺破天穹大地，
刺伤了巴那姆赫赫，
钻进巴那姆赫赫肚子里。
她自生自育，
生出无数跟她一样的怪神。
它就是九头恶魔神
是无往不胜的耶鲁里大神。
它性淫暴烈，
能化气升天，
能化光入日，

能凭角入地，

对三女神毫不惧畏，

反而欺凌侮辱诸女神。

巴那姆赫赫再不能宁静酣眠了，

耶鲁里大神闹得她

肌残肤破，

地动山摇，

地水横溢；

闹得风雷四震，

日月无光，

飞星（流星）满天，

万物惨亡。

Chapter IV

How was the earliest demon born to the world?

Who was the most fiendish demon in the world?

Goddess Aoqin had nine heads,

Who could:

Think much more than all birds and animals,

See with open eyes,

Hear with sharp ears,

Smell with sensitive noses,

And eat with greedy mouths,

All the time.

Therefore,

She learned all wisdom and capability

From the birds and the beasts.

Since she had to shake Banamuhehe awake

Constantly with hands,

She became so physically strong

That she could even rock mountains.

Since she had to attend upon Banamuhehe,

All the time,

She felt bored to the extreme,

And once in a while would roar with rage.

Since her body was made from

The floating clouds and raging flame
That Abukahehe and Woleduohehe had exhaled,
She awfully disturbed Banamuhehe's peace and quiet.
Disgusted with Goddess Aoqin,
Manamuhehe flied into a rage,
Threw out of herself
Two big pinnacle rocks towards Aoqin,
One of which became a horn on Aoqin's head,
Rising straight up into the sky;
One of which stuck into Aoqin's belly,
Turning into a suosuo.
Hit by the two pinnacle rocks,
Goddess Aoqin changed in shape at once,
Turning into a bisexual monster.
With one horn, nine heads and eight arms.
Having a suosuo of her own,
She could conceive and reproduce on her own;
In addition to the bones, flesh and souls
From Abukahehe, Woleduohehe and Banamuhehe,
She had also got
Nine heads to learned all skills and abilities,
One horn that might pierce the sky and the earth,
With which she stabbed Banamuhehe,
And bolted into her belly.
Profane and violent by nature,

The nine-head demon gods,

The invincible God Yeluli,

Conceived and reproduced on her own,

Creating a myriad of evil spirits just like her.

Changing into air,

It could rise up into heaven;

Changing into light,

It could melt into the sun;

With the horn,

It could drill into the earth.

In no fear of the three goddesses at all,

It bullied and humiliated them instead.

Banamuhehe could no more enjoy

Her quiet and sound sleep,

Since God Yeluli put her into such an mess that,

The earth trembled,

The mountains swayed,

Her skin was severely fractured,

And the earth was catastrophically flooded.

What was worse,

Wind roared and thunder rumbled in all directions,

The sun and the moon dimmed day and night,

Flying stars [shooting stars] crossed over the sky,

And all creatures died in misery.

伍腓凌

世上最早的鏖战是什么?

世上最惨的拼争是什么?

九头敖钦女神

变成了一角、九头、

自生自育的恶魔耶鲁里,

自恃穹宇无敌,

凌辱三女神。

她知道卧勒多赫赫

有个布星桦皮口袋,

能骗到手就可以独揽星阵,

可吃、住、藏身,

同阿布卡赫赫抗衡无阻。

于是,

她把九个头变成九颗亮星,

像太阳一样光芒四射,

于是天上像有了十个太阳。

阿布卡赫赫和卧勒多赫赫大吃一惊。

卧勒多赫赫忙用桦皮口袋

去装九颗亮星,

亮星装进去了,

刚要背走,

哪知连卧勒多赫赫自身

也给带入地下。
原来口袋套在耶鲁里的九个脑袋上，
耶鲁里力大无比，
卧勒多赫赫成了俘虏。
卧勒多赫赫乃是周行天地的光明神，
与巴那姆赫赫为同根姊妹。
耶鲁里把她囚入地下，
她的光芒照得
耶鲁里九个头上的眼睛失明，
头晕目旋，
慌忙将抓在手上的
布星桦皮口袋抛出来，
正巧是从东往西抛出的，
布星女神卧勒多赫赫
便从东往西追赶，
得到了布星口袋。
从此，
星星总是
从东方升起，
从西方移动，
万年如此，
这就是耶鲁里给抛出来的星移路线。

凶暴的耶鲁里，

搅得天昏地暗，
日、月、星辰黑暗无光。
耶鲁里打败了卧勒多赫赫，
又想征服阿布卡赫赫，
便去找阿布卡赫赫打赌。
狡猾的耶鲁里凭着
九个头上的神眼和
九个头的智谋，
向阿布卡赫赫提出，
看谁最有能耐
寻找到光明，
看谁最先分辨出
天是什么颜色，
地是什么颜色。

耶鲁里凭着恶魔的眼力，
在黑暗的冰块上找到了白冰，
而且理直气壮地说：
“我敢打赌，
天与地都是白色的。”
说着，他让自生自育的
无数耶鲁里，
到遥远的白海，
把冰山搬来。

阿布卡赫赫苦无良策，
处处是白森森的、
凉瓦瓦的、
白茫茫的。
危机时刻，
巴那姆赫赫派去了
身边的九色花翅大嘴巨鸭，
它翅宽蔽海，
鸣如儿啼，
把阿布卡赫赫
从被囚困的冰水中背上蓝天，
躲过了灾难。
但是，
冰海盖住了天穹，
遮盖了大地。
大嘴巨鸭口喷烈火，
把冰天给啄了个洞，
又啄个洞，
一连气儿啄了千千万万个洞。
从此才又出现了日、月、星光，
才有了光明温暖。
可是，
耶鲁里搬来的冰雪总也化不完。
大嘴巨鸭的嘴

最初也是
又尖又宽、
又厚又长的，
像钻镐一般，
就因为援救阿布卡赫赫，
凿冰不息，
大地有了光明，
可鸭嘴却从此以后，
让冰凌巨块给挤压得
又扁又圆了，
双爪也给挤压成三片叶形了。

耶鲁里喷吐黑风恶水，
阿布卡赫赫派身边的
霍洛浑和霍洛昆[1]两个女神详查动静。
他俩只见
寰宇动晃，
天石颓塌，
地陷涌泉，
回去报告阿布卡赫赫，
已经是来不及了，
便放开喉咙大声唱乌春[2]。

1 霍洛浑和霍洛昆：满族创世神话中的歌神。
2 乌春：满语，意为歌。

两个女神边唱边携手舞蹈，
在颓石浪尖上唱，
在恶风凄雨中跳。
歌舞迷住了耶鲁里，
他竟忘了施展雄威，
闭目睡了过去。
等他突然猛醒来时，
阿布卡赫赫已经
率百兽百禽围袭而来。
耶鲁里双手一按，
竟将两个女神
碾成血粉。
后来血粉干润在树草之上，
小小的粉粒化成万千鸣虫，
体小而其声悠亢，
声振数里可闻。
而且声调有
嬉戏、忧思、欢庆、警示、
探询等不同韵味，
显露其被害前，
仍不服耶鲁里的欺凌，
代代年年，
叽叽鸣唱，
为世人警世诵歌。

萨满祝祭时，
常以加昆玛音大萨满临降，
擅歌舞，百虫鸣唱。

在萨哈连之北，
有神山名曼君乌延哈达。
其峰尖在云际，
山中终年存雪，
唯夏间融化成溪，
湍流声啸数十里。
射猎、打渔、捕貉鹰之属
皆以曼君乌延之雪，
度卜天年。
天穹初开时，
阿布卡赫赫与耶鲁里争雄，
此山为卧勒多赫赫
布星阵中之巨星，
称寒星，
或称雪星，
住有曼君女神，
又称曼君额云[1]，
曼君实为尼莽吉，
即为雪也，

1　额云：满语，意为姐姐。

也就是雪神所居之神星。
在阿布卡赫赫与耶鲁里搏拼时，
阿布卡赫赫猛力一踩，
因为身子被耶鲁里恶魔压住，
喘不过气来，
猛力一挣，
只听轰隆隆一声，
将雪星踏裂，
天上留下一半，
掉到地上一半。
从此以后，
雪神分两地居住，
在天上居住时，
北方无雪，
春暖花开；
在地上居住时，
北方沃雪连年，
洁白连天如银界。
掉在地上这一半星星，
便是北方的曼君乌延哈达。
因为雪神一年两居，
凡雪神居于天上时，
此地便为春天；
雪神返回地上时，

此地便是冬天。
所以，
此山又名宁摄里神山，
以此神山确定北方的季节。
曼君乌延女神，
是季节神，
又是北方雪神，
年年致祭不衰。

阿布卡赫赫身边
第三个侍女叫奥朵西，
意为小姑娘，
掌握七彩云兽，
是放云马的神女。
天河中的各色云兽，
都是按奥朵西的意愿奔行。
有的像虎，
有的像豹，
有的像鹿，
有的像兔，
有的像马，
有的像猪，
变幻无穷。
阿布卡赫赫追赶耶鲁里，

总是追不上。
奥朵西便想出一个
巧妙的招法，
用藤草编成白色的马，
借给耶鲁里。
耶鲁里挺高兴，
哪知骑上白马便被藤草缠住。
耶鲁里这才被阿布卡赫赫捉住，彻底服输。
耶鲁里说了软话，
阿布卡赫赫心慈手软，
放了他。
不料，
耶鲁里马上就变心了，
还照样伤害生灵。
耶鲁里见阿布卡赫赫
身披九彩云光衫，
姿貌秀美，
便想调戏她，
并想得到她。
阿布卡赫赫格外恼火，
一见到耶鲁里就头发涨，
看不清楚耶鲁里的全身，
只见到他的九个脑袋，
便头昏目眩，

忙让众侍女轰走他。
大侍女喜鹊用叫声赶走他，
耶鲁里用几座山塞住了耳朵；
二侍女用刺猬针上的太阳光
刺他的九头双眼，
耶鲁里用白雾作眼帘；
三侍女奥朵西便将七彩云马
赶进了耶鲁里的眼睛里，
耶鲁里疼得双目一十八只眼睛，
都变成了黑雾，有如
被赶跑了。
可是耶鲁里的眼睛
裹走了许多天马，
天的颜色从此不再是九个颜色，
而变成七色了。
阿布卡赫赫非常生气，
将奥朵西赶走，
不准她再做牧兽女神。
可是奥朵西走后，
天上又少了百兽的
蹄声、叫声，
天空只有一片云光。
阿布卡赫赫深感寂寞，
便又把小奥朵西召到身边，

重做牧神。
奥朵西是智慧的战神，
所以各族敬尊奥朵西为
牧神和侍家女神，
庇佑宅室女红顺遂。
神偶供于堂屋的正北方。

在萨哈连极北地方，
是一片千年松林和古岩幽洞，
有七座山头连为一体，
并峙入天，
称穆丹阿林。
四周群山围拥，
白云护庇，
百兽繁居，
鸣唱如神界。
其山多异禽异兽，
生九彩斑纹鸟，
其声如女儿语，
又有双头七彩花节蛇，
有此蛇处可得七星翡翠，
为玉宝。
北人多跋涉千里，
采玉易货于南方。

相传，

天命初，

宫妃多赐用穆丹玉。

穆丹阿林，

阿布卡赫赫在驱赶

恶魔耶鲁里时，

从自己头上摘下玉坠，

打向耶鲁里，

耶鲁里的头被打掉了一颗

掉在此地，

那块玉坠也被打碎，

落在耶鲁里掉下来的头上，

变成了一座玉石山，

包围住了那颗魔头。

可是耶鲁里神技无敌，

马上将掉下头的那个地方，

一连凸出六个同样的大山。

阿布卡赫赫和巴那姆赫赫

来找那颗魔头，

已经难以觅寻，

在七个大山和周围的小山丘中，

无法再找到耶鲁里的头。

耶鲁里从地下

偷偷把那颗头找到

安到了自己的身上。

从此，

这里出现了七座大山，

而且山中多奇玉，

都是阿布卡赫赫

头上的玉坠化成的。

山中多幽洞，

是阿布卡赫赫派诸神

捉拿魔头，

给钻拱出来的，

幽洞甚深长，

多冰瀑、潜流，

多蟒、豹等猛兽。

穆丹阿林与摄力神山，

同为北方诸族致祭的名山。

长途献牲、

祝祭者

从春走到冬，

由冬走到春，

骑马、步行，

赶着勒勒车向北虔诚进发，

逶迤不绝。

清初仍不绝于道。

在萨哈连以北，
穆丹阿林以东，
还有个著名的玛呼山，
也是这一带诸族人常祭的神山。
相传，
这个山为“天宫大战”时，
阿布卡赫赫率领
众动植大神，
打败了九头恶魔耶鲁里，
将他烧化成一个九头的小鸟，
打入地心之中，
永不能残害寰宇。
神火燔烧耶鲁里的魔骨，
从天上掉到了这里，
变成了一条绵延的
白骨、乌骨、
绿骨、黄骨
堆成的石山，
其山中石木皆为
此骨诸种颜色，
并有灵气。
萨满千里北上
采集灵石灵佩，
均要攀登玛呼山，

即瞒盖山，

也称魔骨山。

在萨满诸姓的神物中，

神裙、神帽、

神鞭、神碗

都有用到玛呼山的玛呼石

磨制神奇的器物。

萨满还用此

石板、石盅、

石柱、石针

占卜医病，

成为萨满重要的

灵验的神物。

阿布卡赫赫，

所造的敖钦女神，

是为了守侍巴那姆赫赫，

使她不能安眠昏睡。

阿布卡赫赫又觉得

只让敖钦女神守护，

还不放心。

敖钦女神九头八臂，

神力盖世，

一旦逃跑，

就会变成无敌于世的
宇内大神。
便又派出看门的都凯女神，
并告诫她要时时关好天门，
让敖钦女神只能在
神域之内活动，
不能随意出走。
敖钦女神有九个头，
敏慧无匹，
便把憨厚的都凯女神骗来，
同她戏耍，
共同筑建地穴住室。
敖钦女神把头上的触角
借给都凯女神用来钻地穴行。
都凯女神甚觉好玩，
敖钦女神由此才冲出天门，
成为神威齐天的耶鲁里。
阿布卡赫赫大怒，
把都凯女神赶出天系。
巴那姆赫赫怜悯她，
便将都凯女神收留，
平时让她变成蚯蚓，
总是穿行地穴，
决意要寻找耶鲁里，

以雪渎职之恨，
从此她无颜见天上太阳，
太阳一照便会死去。
所以北方诸族的人，
在萨满的服饰上
常画有蛇状虫，
有些并不是蛇
也不是龙，
而是蚯蚓。
相传，
它有耶鲁里的触角，
可穿行于地下，
能够辅助与导引萨满
探查地下的府洞与魂魄，
畅行无阻。

都凯女神变成地下蚯蚓，
永远不能生活于地上，
但她常常帮助
阿布卡赫赫的护眼女神。
护眼女神的神火能透穿大地，
润育沃野，
可以孳生万物。
都凯女神为了能回到

阿布卡赫赫身边，
便竭力帮助护眼女神，
把深深的地层
钻出洞眼，
使暖光透进，
使她能够随时幻化成
各种香花异草。
护眼女神后来能变成
芍丹乌西哈，
使耶鲁里上当，
救了阿布卡赫赫
也有都凯女神的功劳。
阿布卡赫赫怜爱都凯女神，
允许她可以自生自育，
不论冬夏她永远不死，
常存于地下。
蚯蚓神又称小蟒神，
可助萨满治世宁人。

Chapter V

What was the first war in the world?
What was the most brutal fight in the world?
Nine-head Goddess Aoqin
turned into the one-horn, nine-head,
Self-reproductive demon Yeluli,
Who insulted the three goddesses,
And boasted of being invincible in the universe.
She knew
Woleduohehe had got a star-scattering birch-bark bag;
If she stole it,
She could not merely monopolize all stars,
But also eat, live and hide in it,
And rival Abukahehe with ease.
Therefore,
She disguised her nine heads into nine bright stars,
Brilliant as the sun,
As if there were ten suns in the sky,
Which greatly shocked Abukahehe and Woleduohehe.
Woleduohehe hurriedly
Held the nine bright stars into her birch-bark bag;
Just when she was about to carry them away,
She was suddenly dragged underground;

It turned out the bag was put on Yeluli's nine heads.
Unable to match Yeluli in physical strength,
Woleduohehe was taken as a captive.
As the Light Goddess between the heaven and the earth,
Woleduohehe was the same-rooted sister with Banamuhehe;
Though Yeluli trapped her into underground,
Her brilliant rays were so harsh
That they blinded Yeluli's eyes in his nine heads,
Making him dizzy.
In haste,
He flung out with his hands
The star-scattering birch bark bag,
Which happened to move from east to west;
Seeing that,
Woleduohehe, the Star Goddess,
Chased after it from east to west,
And finally caught it.
From then on,
Stars,
Invariably rose in the east,
And moved to the west,
Which followed the star moving track
That was set by Yeluli's fling direction,
Year after year.

The fierce and brutal Yeluli,
Stirred up chaos all around,
Leaving the heaven gloomy and the earth dark,
Making the sun, the moon and the stars dim.
After defeating Woleduohehe,
Yeluli intended to conquer Abukahehe,
Thus he went to Abukahehe for a bet.
With the eyes in his nine heads
And more resourcefulness in his nine brains
Crafty Yeluli wagered with Abukahehe on
Who was the most capable of finding brightness;
Who was the first to tell
What color the sky was,
And what color the earth was.

Yeluli took advantage of his devil eyesight to
Find a piece of white ice on the dark ice block,
And asserted with self-confidence:
"I bet,
The heaven and the earth are all in white."
With that,
He ordered his countless self-reproduced Yelulies
To carry an iceberg from the remote White Sea.

Abukahehe was at a total loss,
Leaving the whole world in
Stark pale,
Utterly cold,
And endlessly gloomy white.
At the critical moment,
Banamuhehe sent there
Her nine-color-wing, big-beak giant duck,
Whose wings were so wide that they cover the sea,
Whose twitter sounded so sharp like baby cry,
To rescue and take Abukahehe back to the heaven,
Saving her from the catastrophe.
However,
The frozen sea covered the sky,
And blanketed the earth.
The big-beak duck spit fire from its mouth,
Pecking holes in the frozen sky,
One after another,
Tens of thousands at a stretch.
From then on, there came
The sun,
The moon,
The stars,
And thus light and warmth.

Yet the ice and snow that moved by Yeluli,
Would never melt away.
Originally,
The beak of the big-beak duck had been
Sharp and broad,
Thick and long,
Just like a pickaxe;
But in order to rescue Abukahehe,
It drilled the ice without cease,
So the light could reach the earth.
From then on,
The duck's beak was compressed flat and round
By the big ice blocks,
And its two claws were squeezed into
The three-leaf shape.

Yeluli blew black wind and sprayed evil rain,
So Abukahehe sent two of the goddesses at her side,
Huoluohun and Huoluokun[1],
To see what happened.
They saw
The whole world was shaking,
The celestial stones were collapsing,

---

1 Huoluohun and Huoluokun:The goddesses of song in creation myth of Manchu.

The earth was sinking down,
While water were welling up.
Too late for them
To return and inform Abukahehe of the situation,
They raised their voice and sang wuchun songs with full throat.
Two goddesses kept singing and dancing hand in hand,
Singing on the top of dilapidated rock and wave,
Dancing in the evil wind and chilling rain.
Charmed by their singing and dancing,
Yeluli forgot to cast evil spells,
Closed his eyes and fell into a sleep.
When he woke up all of a sudden,
Abukahehe had laid siege with all beasts and birds.
With his two giant hands,
Yeluli crushed the two goddesses
Into blood powder.
Later the blood powder dried
Covered the trees and grass,
And turned into thousands of buzzing insects,
Who were small in size,
But strong in sound,
And could be heard miles away.
In addition,
their tones contained various emotions like

Frolic, sorrow,

Celebration, alarm and inquiry,

Which revealed

They would never yield to Yeluli's bullying

In the face of death and persecution.

They kept chirping,

Singing to warn the world,

Year after year,

Generation after generation.

When blessing the sacrifice,

Shamans usually performed

In the form of Shaman Jiakunmayin,

Who was good at singing, dangcing

And imitating the sound of insects.

To the north of Sahalian River,

There was a holy mountain,

Named Manjun Wuyanhada.

Its jutting peaks were so high,

That they could touch the clouds;

Snow and ice in the mountains

Remained all year round,

But melted into a stream only in summer,

With turbulent rapids roaring

Tens of miles away.
Livelihood such as
Hunting, fishing, catching raccoons and eagles
All counted on
The snow in Mountain Manjun Wuyanhada
To predict the year's harvest.
In the beginning of heaven formation,
When Abukahehe and Yeluli fought for supremacy,
This mountain was a giant star named Cold Star,
Also known as Snow Star,
That belonged to Woleduohehe's star array;
On the star lived Goddess Manjun,
Named Manjun Eyun[1].
Manjun actually was Nimangji,
Namely, the snow;
Thus the Cold Star was a holy star
For the Snow Goddess.
While Abukahehe was fighting with Yeluli,
She stamped with a sudden force;
As she was pinned down by Yeluli,
And could hardly breathe,
She tried to free herself with great effort.
All of a sudden,

1 Eyun:Manchu language, sister.

With a loud boom of thundered,
She split the Snow Star with a violent stamp,
One half hanging in the sky,
The other falling onto the earth.
From then on,
The Snow Goddess took residence
In two places by turns.
When she lived in the sky,
There was no snow in the north,
But spring blossoms everywhere;
When she lived on the earth,
The north was covered with
Thick snow all year round,
Pure and white everywhere,
Like a silver world reaching the sky.
Half of the star that fell on the earth,
Was the Manjun Wuyanhada.
Since the Snow Goddess
Resided in two dwellings a year,
When she lived in the sky,
The spring approached;
When she returned to the earth,
The winter started.
Therefore,

The mountain was also known as
Mountain Ningsheli,
Which determineed the seasons in the north.
Goddess Manjun Wuyan,
The Goddess of Seasons,
Meanwhile the Snow Goddess of the north,
Was worshiped year after year.

By the side of Abukahehe,
The third maid was named Aoduoxi,
Meaning "little girl";
She was in charge of seven-color-cloud beasts,
And herded the cloud horses.
All the cloud beasts in the Milky Way,
Were moving in accordance with Aoduoxi's wishes:
Some of them looked like tigers,
Some of them looked like leopards,
Some of them looked like deer,
Some of them looked like rabbits,
Some of them looked like horses,
Some of them looked like pigs,
And all transformed in various shapes and sizes.
Abukahehe tried to catch up with Yeluli,
But in vain.

Aoduoxi came up with an ingenious trick.
She weaved rattan into a white horse,
And lent it to Yeluli.
Yeluli was very happy;
But not until he mounted the horse
Was he entangled in the rattan.
Finally Yeluli was caught by Abukahehe,
And admitted defeat.
But when Yeluli spoke some soft words,
Abukahehe grew softhearted,
Thus released him.
However,
Yeluli changed his mind soon,
And tormented all creatures as usual.
Yeluli saw Abukahehe
Wearing nine-color cloud-light garment,
Beautiful and graceful in appearance,
So he attempted to molest her,
And intended to get her.
Abukahehe grew annoyed in the extreme.
At sight of Yeluli,
She felt sickened;
At sight of his nine heads,
She felt dizzy.

Thus she urged the maids to drive him off.
The First Maid Magpie tried to
Chase him away by squeaking,
But Yeluli stuffed his ears with mountains;
The Second Maid attempted to
Blind the eyes on his nine heads
With the sunlight from the hedgehog spine,
But Yeluli used white mist as protective shield;
Finally,
The Third Maid Oduoxi
Drove the seven-color cloud-horses into Yeluli's eyes.
Suffering from the intense pain of his eighteen eyes,
Which were much hurt by dark mist and bug bite,
Yeluli was driven off.
However,
Yeluli's eyes whirled away
So many colorful-cloud horses,
That the sky was no longer nine colors,
But turned into seven colors.
Abukahehe grew so mad,
That she drove Aoduoxi off,
Depriving her of the title of
Goddess of Mythical Beasts.
However,

Since Aoduoxi left,

There were no more beasts in the heaven,

No more running hoof beats,

Or whinnying cries,

But a glow of cloud light.

Desperately lonely,

Abukahehe recalled little Aoduoxi,

And reappointed her as Herding Goddess.

Auduoxi was an intelligent Goddess of War,

So people of all tribes adored her as

Herding Goddess and Home Guarding Goddess,

Who guarded the house,

And blessed women with good fortune.

Her holy image was enshrined

In the north of the central room.

In the far north of Sahalian,

There was a pine forest of one thousand years old,

And numerous ancient caves.

Among them were seven continuous mountain peaks,

Standing upright to the sky,

Which were called Mudan'alin.

Surrounded by mountains,

Sheltered by white clouds,

With all animals living and singing,
It was like a divine world.
The mountains were rich in rare fowls and beasts,
One of which was a nine-color-stripe bird,
Whose singing was like girl's sweet voice;
One of which was a two-head seven-color snake,
In whose habitat there was seven-star jade,
The jade of treasure.
The northerners traveled a long distance,
Mined the jade and bartered it in Nanming.
Legend has it that,
At the beginning of heaven formation,
The royal princesses were bestowed Mudan jade.
When chasing the devil Yeluli,
Abukahehe picked off a jade pendant from her hair,
Threw it at Yeluli,
And knocked off one of his heads
Down to the ground.
The jade pendant was broken,
Falling down on Yeluli's head,
Then turned into a jade mountain,
Encircling the devil head,
Which became the Mudan'alin.
However,

Yeluli was so invincibly powerful in magic,
That he quickly conjured other six identical mountains,
Right at the spot his head fell.
When Abukahehe and Banamuhehe
Came searching for his head,
It was definitely impossible to retrieve it,
In the seven high mountains,
And numerous hills around.
Secretly from underground,
Yeluli somehow found his missing head,
And placed it back on his neck.
Since then,
There turned up seven high mountains,
With plenty of rare jade,
Which transformed from the jade pendant
On Abukahehe's head.
In the mountains,
There formed many deep caves,
Which were drilled and pushed through,
When Abukahehe sent all goddess
To seize the devil head.
The caves were deep and long,
With many icefalls, streams,
Pythons, leopards and other beasts.

Mudan'alin and Sheli Holy Mountain,
Both were famous mountains
For northern tribes to worship.
To offer sacrifices far away,
The worshipers travelled,
Over mountains and rivers,
From spring to winter,
And winter to spring;
Some rode horses,
Some walked,
Some drove Lele cart to the north,
Like an endless stream,
All with religious hearts.
It still prevailed in early Qing Dynasty.

To the north of Sahalian,
To the east of Mudan'alin,
There was a famous Mahu Mountain,
A holy mountain for local tribes to worship.
Legend has it that,
The mountain could even trace back to
The time of "the War of Creation",
When Abukahehe commanded
All animal and plant goddesses,

Defeated the nine-head devil Yeluli,
Incinerated him into a nine-head little bird,
And banished him into the earth's core,
So he could never harm the world any more.
The sacred fire incinerated Yeluli's devil bones
Into a stretch of rocky mountains,
Where was stacked of bones of
White, black, green and yellow.
All stones and plants in the mountains
Shared same color with the bones,
And sprouted out spirituality.
To collect the spiritual stones and jades,
Shamans would
Trek from thousands of miles away to the north,
And climbed up Mahu Mountain,
Namely, Mangai Mountain,
Or Devil Bone Mountain.
Among the religious artifacts of all Shaman tribes,
Magical skirts, magical hats,
Magical whips and magical bowls
Were all magical instruments
Made of Mahu stones from Mahu Mountain.
Shaman used these
Stone slabs and stone cups,

Stone pillars and stone needles,
To practice divination and medicine,
Which were Shaman's most important
And efficacious religious artifacts.

Abukahehe created Goddess Aoqin,
In hope that she could
Guard and attend upon Banamuhehe,
Prevent her from sound sleep.
Somehow Abukahehe felt it unreliable
To merely send Goddess Aoqin there.
Goddess Aoqin had nine heads, eight arms,
And extraordinary strength;
Once escaping,
She would turn into
An invincible super god of the universe.
Therefore,
She sent there Goddess Dukai, a gate guardian,
Commanding her to ensure
The heaven gate was closed all the time,
So that Goddess Aoqin could only
Hang around within the spirit world,
But could not get out of the bounds at will.
Goddess Aoqin had nine heads,

Making her unparalleled in wits;
Thus she cheated the simple and honest Goddess Dukai
To play with her,
And built an underground accommodation together.
Goddess Aoqin lent Goddess Dukai the horn,
With which she could
drill the earth and move about underground;
Goddess Dukai felt it extremely interesting,
And so was addicted to it.
Thus Goddess Aoqin rushed out of the heaven gate,
And became the invincible mighty Yeluli.
Flying into a rage,
Abukahehe drove Goddess Dukai out of the heaven.
Having a pity on her,
Banamuhehe took Goddess Dukai in,
Changing her into an earthworm,
Who moved about underground all the time,
Resolved to find out Yeluli,
And took revenge for the insult of malpractice.
Since then,
She felt ashamed to look up into the sun,
And would die from exposure to the sunlight.
So people of northern tribes,
Often drew onto Shaman's costumes

Some snake-shaped worms,
Which were not snakes or dragons at all,
But the earthworms.
Legend has it that,
Earthworms had got Yeluli's horn,
Thus they could move through underground,
Assist and guide Shaman
To explore the caves and the spirits underground,
Without hindrance.

Though Goddess Dukai
Changed into an earthworm underground,
Unable to live above the ground ever since,
She often helped Abukahehe's Eye Protecting Goddess.
The holy fire of the Eye Protecting Goddess could
Penetrate through the earth,
Fertilize over the field,
Create and grow all creatures on the earth.
To return to Abukahehe's side,
Goddess Dukai spared no effort to
Help the Eye Protecting Goddess,
And drilled holes in deep layers of the earth,
So the warm light could penetrate,
And the Eye Protecting Goddess could turn into

Various fragrant flowers and rare grasses.
Later the Eye Protecting Goddess
Turned into Peony Wuxiha,
Seized Yeluli and rescued Abukahehe,
Which was partially attributed to Goddess Dukai's merits.
Abukahehe showed mercy to Goddess Dukai,
Allowing her to grow and self-reproduce,
Never die whether in summer or winter,
And live underground forever.
Hence,
The Goddess Earthworm was also known as
Goddess Litter Snake,
Who could help Shaman to
Rule the world and cure the people.

陆腓凌

世上谁是长生不死的神？
谁是不可抗争的大神？
九头恶魔耶鲁里
率领自生自育的成千的恶魔，
吞噬万物，
称霸苍穹，
浊雾弥天，
禽兽丧亡。
可是，
耶鲁里的九头八臂都能裂生出恶魔，
眼睛可生恶魔，
耳朵可生恶魔，
汗毛孔里都能钻出
小小的耶鲁里模样的恶魔，
像蝼蚁，
像蜂群，
齐向阿布卡赫赫围击。
阿布卡赫赫杀死了
一群又一群，
耶鲁里连生不灭，
恶魔反倒比以前更凶更多。
在分不清天

分不清地的时候，
有个多喀霍神出现了。
这位女神就是以石为屋，
永久住在巴那姆赫赫
肤体的石头里的神。
她能帮助众神
获得生命和力量，
并有自育自生的能力。
她听说九头恶魔耶鲁里
在天穹大显神威，
阿布卡赫赫、巴那姆赫赫
对其也无可奈何，
天昏地暗。
巴那姆赫赫肤体
被其触角豁伤，
伤痕累累；
阿布卡赫赫肤体
也被触角搅得
飞星落地、
白云不生。
七彩神光被其九头遮盖，
只能见到红色和黑色。
见到世上恶魔逞凶，
多噜霍神便和阿布卡赫赫身边的

西斯林女神商量

让西斯林女神施展风威，

用飞沙走石驱赶恶魔。

西斯林女神是

阿布卡赫赫的爱女，

生下来就神威无比，

而且是穹宇中的力神，

是卧勒多赫赫的两只大脚。

阿布卡赫赫，

就是用卧勒多赫赫身上、

脚上的肉，

和她的慈肉，

合成的敖钦女神。

所以，敖钦女神能巡行大地，

不知疲累。

敖钦女神变成了

九头恶魔耶鲁里后，

耶鲁里因身上有

卧勒多赫赫脚上的肉，

因此也具有摇撼世界的风力，

力大无穷，

疾行如闪。

但耶鲁里终究比不上

西斯林女神威武有力，

因她统管天宇的风气，
欲小则小，
欲大则大，
所以能背得动
装满星云的桦皮口袋。
西斯林女神
见到阿布卡赫赫被困，
便同意多喀霍女神的请求，
搬运巴那姆赫赫肤体上的巨石，
追打魔群耶鲁里们。

耶鲁里在得意志满时，
突然遭到满天飞来的巨石击打，
无处藏身，
便仓惶逃回到地下，
暂躲起来，
天穹才又现出光明。
耶鲁里不甘心，
又去找阿布卡赫赫说：
“你若是敢跟我比试飞速，
若是你超过我、
追过我，
我就服输，
再不扰乱苍穹，

情愿做你顺从的侍卫。”
阿布卡赫赫心想：
任你怎么飞跳，
也跳不出我的肤体之外，
又有两个妹妹女神从旁辅佑，
我们必能俘获你。
便同意跟耶鲁里比试高低。
聪明狡猾的九头恶魔耶鲁里，
有九个头的智慧，
九双眼睛的目光，
又有三个女神的神力，
听了非常高兴，
暗想，
阿布卡赫赫你可上了当。
两人约好，
开始比试飞力。
耶鲁里化光而逝，
阿布卡赫赫凭着
七彩神火照射，
早看得清楚，
便追了下去。
耶鲁里生性能够自生自育，
化成无数个耶鲁里。
阿布卡赫赫认不出

哪一个是耶鲁里的正身，
遥望前头有个又高又粗的
九头耶鲁里模样的恶魔，
超过其他耶鲁里，
心想这回可算盯住了，
决不能再让耶鲁里藏身。
追啊追，
九头耶鲁里一下钻进白雾里，
阿布卡赫赫刚要抓住
耶鲁里的一个头，
便觉周身寒冷沉重，
一座座大雪山
压到阿布卡赫赫身上。
耶鲁里把阿布卡赫赫
骗进了北天雪海里逃走了。
雪海里的雪山堆得比天还高，
压得阿布卡赫赫冻饿难忍。
这里是雪山底下的石堆，
里边住着多喀霍女神，
温暖着阿布卡赫赫的身躯。
阿布卡赫赫饿得没有办法，
又无法脱身，
只好在雪山底下
啃着巨石充饥。

阿布卡赫赫把山岩里的巨石
都吞进了腹内，
顿觉周身发热。
因为多喀霍女神
是光明和火的化身，
热力烧得阿布卡赫赫
坐立不安，
浑身充满了巨力，
烤化了雪山，
一下子又重新撞开
层层雪海雪山，
冲上穹宇。
可是热火烧得阿布卡赫赫
肢身融解，
眼睛分别变成了日、月，
头发变成了森林，
汗水变成了溪河……
所以，后世都讲，
地上的森林、湖海、河流，
不少是从天上掉下来的。
不单是山林、溪流，
阿布卡赫赫与耶鲁里搏斗，
扰得天空不宁，
也把不少生物从天上挤下来。

蛇就是光神的化身，
是从天上掉下来的，
虫类也是从天上掉下来的。
所以它们在有火和光的春夏
才能出洞生活，
在无火无光的暗夜和严冬
便入眠了。

Chapter VI

Who was the immortal god in the world?
Who was the invincible god in the world?
The nine-head Devil Yeluli
Commanded thousands of devils he reproduced,
Devoured all things and dominated the universe,
Leaving the sky full of blushing fog,
Making birds and animals dying out.
However,
Yeluli's nine heads and eight arms
Could reproduce devils:
From his eyes came out devils;
From his ears came out devils;
From his sweat pores came out
Little Yeluli-like devils;
Like the ants,
Like the bees,
They all swarmed up and besieged Abukahehe.
Abukahehe killed the devils
Group after group,
While Yeluli reproduced constantly.
Worse still,
The devils were more fierce and numerous than ever.

At the critical moment,

When it was hard to

Tell between the heaven and the earth,

Goddess Duokehuo emerged.

The Goddess took stones for house,

Permanently residing in the stones

Of Banamuhehe's skin.

She could help all gods to gain life and power,

And was capable of self-fertility.

She heard that nine-head devil Yeluli

Was showing off his magic power in the heaven,

Leaving the world gloomy above and dark below,

So that Even Abukahehe and Banamuhehe

Felt desperately helpless.

Banamuhehe's skin

Was split open by the horn,

Black and blue all over;

Abukahehe's skin

Was injured by the horn,

With flying stars falling down to the ground,

And white clouds fading away.

The sacred seven-color light

Was covered up by the nine heads,

Leaving only black and red visible.

Seeing that devils ran amuck in the world,
Goddess Duokehuo consulted with Goddess Xisilin
Who was at the side of Abukahehe,
Telling her to put the wind strength to the full,
And drove devils away with flying sand and rolling stones.
Born with extraordinary power,
Known as Goddess of Strength,
Goddess Xisilin was Abukahehe's beloved daughter,
Who served as Woleduohehe's two giant feet.
Abukahehe,
Combined the flesh from Woleduohehe's body and feet
With her own kind flesh,
And created the Goddess Aoqin.
Consequently,
Goddess Aoqin could travel throughout the earth,
Never feeling fatigue.
Because Aoqin was made of the flesh
From Woleduohehe's feet,
When changing into
The nine-head Devil Yeluli all of sudden,
He was as strong as an ox,
As agile as lightning,
And possessed the wind strength
That even could shake the world.

However,

Yeluli was no match for Goddess Xisilin in strength,

Who was in charge of winds and currents in the universe;

Turning tiny at will,

Turning giant at will,

She could carry

The birch-bark bag stuffed with stars and clouds.

Seeing that Abukahehe was trapped,

Goddess Xisilin agreed to Goddess Duokehuo's request,

Moved away the giant rock on Banamuhehe's body,

And Chased away swarms of devil Yelulies.

While Yeluli grew dizzy with success,

Suddenly he was hit by

Huge rocks flying from the sky.

Nowhere to hide himself,

He fled underground in panic,

Sheltering himself for the moment.

Thus the brightness returned in the sky.

Not taking his defeat lying down,

Yeluli went to Abukahehe and said:

"If you dare to race against me in flying,

If you could exceed me,

And catch up with me,

I would admit defeat,

Never create disturbance any more,

And serve as your obedient bodyguard willingly."

Abukahehe thought to herself:

"No matter how fast and high you leap or fly,

You could never escape out of my body;

Besides,

I had two sister goddesses to assist me,

Surely we can win and capture you!"

Therefore,

She embraced his request for competition.

Possessed of the wits of nine heads,

The sight of nine pairs of eyes,

And the magic power from three goddesses,

Clever and crafty nine-head devil Yeluli

Became happy and said to himself,

"Abukahehe, finally you fall into my trap."

Soon they reached an agreement on a flying race.

Changing into light,

Yeluli instantly flashed away,

While by virtue of the ray of seven-color magic fire,

Abukahehe saw him clearly with ease,

And chased after him.

Born with the capability of self-fertility,

Yeluli changed into numerous Yelulies.
Hard for Abukahehe to tell which was the real one,
She suddenly spotted in the distance
The strong and tall figure of nine-head Yeluli,
Flying beyond other Yelulies;
She said to herself to keep a close watch,
And wouldn't let Yeluli go and hide again.
Abukahehe chased and chased;
When she saw nine-head Yeluli bolting into white mist,
She tried to grab one of his heads,
Yet felt cold and heavy all over at once,
With numerous snow mountains falling on her.
Yeluli tricked Abukahehe
Into the snow land of the North Pole,
And then slipped away.
The snow mountains on the snow land
Were far higher than the sky,
Which made it too cold and hungry
For Abukahehe to endure.
Fortunately,
In the rocks beneath the snow mountains,
Lived Goddess Duokehuo,
Who kept warming Abukahehe's body.
Extremely hungry,

Unable to get free,
Abukahehe had to relieve her hunger
By gnawing the huge rocks
Beneath the snow mountains.
After swallowing all the huge rocks,
Abukahehe immediately felt hot all over.
Goddess Duokehuo was
The embodiment of brightness and fire,
Whose heat burned Abukahehe so fiercely
That she felt Restless,
Full of huge strength;
Gradually she melted the Snow Mountains,
Suddenly broke the layers of Snow Sea and mountains,
And rushed back into the sky.
But the hot fire burned Abukahehe so fiercely that
Her limbs melted,
Her eyes turned into the Sun and the Moon,
Her hair changed into forests,
And her sweat formed into streams and rivers.
Therefore,
Later generations all say,
The forests, lakes, seas and rivers on the earth,
Mainly came from the heaven.
In addition to the forests, streams and rivers,

Because Abukahehe was fighting against Yeluli,
Which threw the heaven into chaos,
Many creatures were shoved down to the earth.
The snake, the embodiment of brightness,
Fell down from the heaven,
And so did the insects and worms.
From then on,
They tended to go out of caves in spring and summer,
When there were fire and light;
And fall asleep at night and in severe winter,
When there were no fire or light.

柒腓凌

世上为啥留下了竿上天灯？

世上为何流传下来爱鲜花的风俗？

卧勒多赫赫被九头耶鲁里打败后，

神光被夺走了大半，

变成非常温顺的天上女神，

除了背着桦皮星袋

蹒跚西行，

默哑无言。

阿布卡赫赫就让

巴那姆赫赫照料她妹妹，

陪她玩耍，

怕她寂寞。

一天，

巴那姆赫赫命三鸟在天呼唱，

天穹才有生气：

夜里沙乌沙[1]号叫，

清晨嘎喽[2]号叫，

傍晚嘎哈[3]号叫，

从此这三种鸟总是轮流呼唱。

---

1 沙乌沙：满语，意为猫头鹰。

2 嘎喽：满语，意为雁。

3 嘎哈：满语，意为乌鸦。

巴那姆赫赫还将长在自己
心上的突姆火神
派到天上卧勒多赫赫身边，
用她的光、毛、火、发帮助赫赫照路。
天上常常见到的闪电，
便是突姆火神的影子。
天上常常掉下些天落石，
便是突姆火神脚上的泥。

九头恶魔耶鲁里，
闯出地窟，
又逞凶到天穹，
它要吃掉阿布卡赫赫和众善神。
耶鲁里喷出的恶风黑雾，
遮住了天穹，
暗里无光，
黑龙似的顶天立地的黑风
卷起了天上的星辰和彩云，
卷走了巴那姆赫赫身上的百兽百禽。
突姆火神临危不惧，
将自己身上的火、光、毛、发，
抛到黑空里，
化成依兰乌西哈[1]、

1　依兰乌西哈：满语，意为三星。

那丹乌西哈[1]、

明安乌西哈[2]、

图门乌西哈[3]，

帮助了卧勒多赫赫布星。

然而，突姆火神却全身赤裸，

变成光秃秃、赤裸裸的白石头，

悬垂在依兰乌西哈星星上，

从东到西悠来悠去。

白石头上还发出微光，

照彻大地和万物，

她用生命的最后火光，

为生灵造福。

南天上三星下边的一颗

闪闪晃晃、忽明忽暗的小星，

就是突姆女神仅有的

微火在闪照，

像天灯照亮穹宇。

后世人把它叫做“车库妈妈”，

即秋千女神，

从此后世才有了

高高的秋千架子，

1　那丹乌西哈：满语，意为七星。
2　明安乌西哈：满语，意为千星。
3　图门乌西哈：满语，意为万星。

吊着绳子，

人头顶鱼油灯荡秋千，

就是纪念和敬祀慈祥而勇于献身的

伟大的突姆女神。

后世在部落城寨上和狍獐皮制成的“撮罗子”前，

立着的白桦高竿上，

或在山顶、高树上

用兽头骨盛满獾、野猪油

点燃照天灯，

岁岁点冰灯、

升篝火照耀黑夜，

就是为了驱吓

独角九头恶魔耶鲁里，

也是为了缅念和祭祷突姆女神。

卧勒多赫赫星袋里的那丹女神，

知道突姆女神光灭星殒，

便也钻出了大星袋，

化成数百个小星星，

如同星星火球，

在九头恶魔耶鲁里

搅黑的穹宇中，

照射光芒。

恶风吹得星球，

忽而尔缩变成圆形，
忽而吹扯成长方形，
不少星光也失去了光明，
后来变成了一窝
长勺形的小星团。
这便是七星那丹那拉呼，
其变成现在的模样，
也是耶鲁里的恶风吹成的，
一直到现在，
由东到西缓缓而行，
成为星阵的领星星神。

在东方天空有个蓝色的草地，
有天禽和百树，
生长繁茂，
其中住着依尔哈女神，
她香气四溢，
是阿布卡赫赫身上的
香肉变成的，
她日夜勤劳，
为苍穹制造香云。
所以，
天的颜色总是清澄无尘，
而且总是清新沁人。

她主要依靠
西斯林女神的风翅扇摇，
才永远清新美丽。
耶鲁里在天上
看到这块秀美的所在，
还见西斯林女神用风翅
抚盖着天上的草地，
里面阳光明媚，
百禽鸣唱。
在黑风恶雾里到处天昏地暗，
唯有这里却是另一个世界，
于是便大声怒吼。
耶鲁里知道这必是阿布卡赫赫
在天上栖居的地方，
暗暗高兴，
乔装成一个赶鹅的老太太，
拄着个木杖吆吆喝喝地走来。
天鹅不怕天风，
将翅一合钻进
草香莺啼的小溪里。
老太太用斗篷把头一裹，
躲过暴风，
也随鹅走到小溪旁。
鹅，最初只是三只，

突然鹅生鹅，

鹅变鹅，

越变越多，

不大会儿功夫遍野全是

白花花、

嘎嘎怪叫的大鹅。

老太太的拐杖

一下子变成开沟镐，

把百树、百草、花坛

都给豁成了山谷深涧。

阿布卡赫赫正安静睡觉，

忽然觉得全身被白网拴着，

越拴越紧。

原来白鹅变成了

拴阿布卡赫赫的白筋绳子，

木拐杖原来正是恶魔耶鲁里

又凶又大的顶天触角，

刺扎得阿布卡赫赫遍体鳞伤。

天上这块秀美的草地

正是阿布卡赫赫变成的，

她想躲过耶鲁里的九头魔眼，

结果被它识破了。

守护阿布卡赫赫的西斯林女神

当时正贪恋睡觉，
只张开着风翅保护着阿布卡赫赫，
没用飓风扇动天魔，
被耶鲁里轻易地破了风阵，
抓住了阿布卡赫赫。

阿布卡赫赫被抓，
天要塌陷了，
天摇地晃，
日月马上暗淡无光。
天上的神禽、
地上的神兽相继死亡，
阿布卡赫赫的两个妹妹
吓得手足无措。
三姊妹同根同存，
若是一个被杀，
两个妹妹也就会随着窒息。
眼看大难临头，
耶鲁里就要执掌穹宇，
众魔手舞足蹈，
争霸天地间的星房地窟。
正在这千钧一发之时，
被白筋绳拴绑的
阿布卡赫赫眼泪化成的溪流旁，

住着者固鲁女神们，

她们是阿布卡赫赫的护眼女神，

守护日月，

使其日夜光照宇宙，

送暖至大地。

所以，

她们身上都有光衫慈魂，

其外形虽然瘦小，

但神威远远高过三位女神身边的

众位保护女神。

她们在溪河旁知道阿布卡赫赫被绑，

天地难维，

便化作了一朵芳香四散、

洁白美丽的芍丹乌西哈[1]，

光芒四射。

九头恶魔耶鲁里

一见这朵奇妙的神花，

爱不释手。

恶魔们争抢着摘白花，

谁知白花突然变成

千条万条光箭，

直射耶鲁里的眼睛，

疼得耶鲁里闭目打滚，

1 芍丹乌西哈：满语，意为芍药星。

吼叫震天，
捂着九头逃回地穴之中。

阿布卡赫赫被拯救了，
天地被拯救了。
阿布卡赫赫、巴那姆赫赫、卧勒多赫赫
一齐感谢者固鲁女神。
者固鲁，
原来是天上的刺猬神，
它满身披有能藏魂魄的光针，
帮助阿布卡三姊妹生育万物，
付给灵魂。
她身上的光彩，
全是日月光芒织成的，
锋利无比，
可使万物万魔双目失明，
黯然失色。

西斯林女神因为贪睡，
惹出大祸，
被三女神驱逐出天地之外，
夺去了她的女性神牌。
西斯林从此改变了神形，
后来成了耶鲁里伙下的

男性野神，
放荡不羁，
驰号天地之间，
撼山摇月，
成为万物之害。

后世人们头上
总喜戴花或头髻插花，
认为可惊退魔鬼。
戴花、插花、贴窗花、雕冰花，
都喜欢用白芍药花。
雪花，也是白色的，
恰是阿布卡赫赫剪成的，
可以驱魔洁世，
保佑代代吉祥。

Chapter VII

Why was the heaven lantern left to the earth?

Why was the custom of loving flowers handed down?

After Woleduohehe was defeated by nine-head Yeluli,

More than half of her sacred light was taken away,

And she became a very docile heaven goddess,

Who carried the birch-bark star bag on the back,

Stumbling to the west all the way,

Silent and speechless.

To take care of her sister Woleduohehe,

Abukahehe asked Banamuhehe

To play with her,

For fear that she felt lonely and bored.

One day,

Three birds were ordered to sing in the sky by Banamuhehe,

So as to liven up the heaven:

At night Shawusha [1] hooted;

At dawn Galou [2]honked;

At dusk Gaha [3] cawed;

Since then,

1 Shawusha: Manchu language, owl.

2 Galou: Manchu language, wild goose.

3 Gaha: Manchu language, crow.

Three birds always sing in turns.
Banamuhehe also sent Fire Goddess Tumu,
A goddess growing in her heart,
To accompany Woleduohehe in the heaven,
To use her light, fur, fire and hair
To illuminated the road for her.
The lightning commonly seen in the sky,
Was the trace of Fire Goddess Tumu.
The rocks usually falling from the sky,
Were the soil from Fire Goddess's feet.

In an attempt to
Swallow up Abukahehe and all good goddesses,
The nine-head devil Yeluli,
Rushed out of his cave,
And acted violently in the heaven.
The evil wind and dark mist blown by Yeluli,
Covered the heaven,
Leaving the world in the dark;
The black-dragon-like evil wind between heaven and earth
Swirled up the stars and colorful clouds in the sky,
And swept away all fowls and beasts
From Abukahehe's body.
Facing danger fearlessly,

Fire Goddess Tumu

Threw her flaming hair up to the dark sky,

Which turned into Yilan Wuxiha [1],

Nadan Wuxiha [2],

Ming'an Wuxiha [3],

Tumen Wuxiha [4],

And helped Woleduohehe with star array disposal.

However,

Naked all over,

Fire Goddess Tumu turned into a barren white rock,

Dangling from Star Yilan Wuxiha,

Swinging from east to west.

From the white rock

Glowed a slight glimmer of light,

Shining over the earth and all creatures;

She used up the last glow of fire in her life,

To benefit the living of all.

The lowest of the Three Stars in the south sky,

The twinkling, flickering little star,

Exactly was Goddess Tumu's sole faint fire,

1 Yilan Wuxiha: Manchu language, three stars.
2 Nadan Wuxiha: Manchu language, seven stars or Big Dipper.
3 Ming'an Wuxiha: Manchu language, thousands of stars.
4 Tumen Wuxiha: Myriads of stars.

Glistening and lighting up the sky like a heaven-lantern.
The later generations called it "Cheku Mama",
Namely, the Goddess of Swing.
From then on,
There was high swing frame with hanging ropes,
And people swang on it with a fish-oil lamp on head,
Just to commemorate and admire Tumu,
A kind, dedicated and great Mother Goddess.
Later,
On the city wall
And in front of "Cuoluozi" made of roe deer skin,
Stood white birch poles;
Or on top of mountains and tall trees,
placed animal's skulls filled with badger oil or wild boar oil;
Heaven lantern, ice lantern and a campfire
Were lit up to illuminate the dark night every year,
In an attempt to
Ward off the one-horn nine-head devil Yeluli,
And commemorate and worship Goddess Tumu.

Learning the news of Goddess Tumu's death,
Goddess Nadan,
Who had been living in Woleduohehe's star bag,
Came out of the big star bag,

And changed into hundreds of little stars,
Like sparking fireballs,
Shining with their full power,
In the dark sky disturbed by nine-head devil Yeluli.
Severe evil wind blew the stars,
Sometimes into a compact circle,
Sometimes into a rectangle;
Many stars dimmed and lost their light,
And finally became
A spoon-like cluster of stars.
This is the Big Dipper, Nadan Nahula,
Whose shape now it appears,
Was blown by the evil wind from Yeluli;
Till now it still moves slowly from east to west,
And establishes itself as
The leading star goddess of the star cluster.

In the east of the heaven
There was a blue meadow,
Where lived heavenly birds and grew lush trees;
There also lived Goddess Yierha,
Who was made of Abukahehe's fragrant flesh,
And suffused an exquisite fragrance all around;
She worked hard day and night,

Making auspicious clouds for the heaven.
Therefore,
The color of the sky was always
Clean and clear,
Fresh and refreshing.
Thanks to Goddess Xisilin's flapping wings,
She could maintain youth and beauty forever.

From the heaven,
Yeluli spotted this beautiful place,
And saw Goddess Xisilin flapping her wings
To cover and caress the heavenly meadow,
Where the Sun was shining brightly,
All birds were singing happily.
Seeing it's gloomy above and dark below,
Black wind blew and evil mist diffused all around,
Which was totally different from that holy world,
He howled with anger.
Realizing it might be
Abukahehe's residence in the heaven,
Yeluli laughed in mind,
disguised himself as an old woman
Who drove a gaggle of geese,
Came staggering and shouting,

With a wooden cane in her hand.

The heavenly geese were not afraid of the wind;

They closed their wings

And dove into the stream,

with fragrant grass and singing birds around.

The old woman wrapped her head with the cloak,

Got away from the storming wind,

And went towards the little stream

Along with the geese.

In the beginning,

There were only three geese;

Then the geese bred more geese,

And geese reproduced more geese,

Whose number multiplied rapidly;

Soon everywhere around

Were the white and quacking geese.

The old woman's walking cane

Suddenly changed into a trenching pickaxe,

Which split the trees, grasslands and flowering meadows

Into deep valleys and canyons.

Sleeping in peace and quiet,

Abukahehe suddenly felt herself

bound up by a white net,

Tighter and tighter.
It turned out that
The white geese changed into
A white-tendon rope binding her up;
The wooden cane was Devil Yeluli's
Big and fierce sky-reaching horn,
With which he pricked Abukahehe
Black and blue all over.
The beautiful meadow in the heaven,
Actually was changed by Abukahehe,
Who had intended to hide from
Yeluli's magic eyes on his nine heads,
But in vain.

Deeply immersed in sleeping at the moment,
Abukahehe's guardian, Goddess Xisilin,
Only stretched her wings to protect Abukahehe,
But didn't blow great wind against the devil,
So Yeluli easily broke the wind array,
And captured Abukahehe.

Since Abukahehe was captured,
The heaven was about to collapse;
The sky shook and the earth quaked intensely,

The sun and the moon dimmed immediately.
The mythical animals
Both in the heaven and on the earth,
Died one after another,
Which scared Abukahehe's two sisters out of wits.
The three sisters were born and existed together;
If one were killed,
The other two would subsequently die of suffocation.
A great calamity was round the corner;
Yeluli was going to control the universe.
All devils leapt with glee,
Scrambled for stars and caves
Between the heaven and the earth.
At such a critical moment,
By the side of tear stream of Abukahehe,
Who was tightly bound by white-goose-tendon rope,
Lived Goddesses Zhegulu.
As Abukahehe's Eye Protecting Goddesses,
She guarded the sun and the moon,
And saw it that
The light could
Illuminate the univer se clay and night,
Give off warmth to the earth.
Therefore,

Tiny as in appearance,
They were possessed of
Light garments and kind souls;
Their magic power were far more stronger than
All guardian goddesses around the three goddesses.
Learning that
Abukahehe was bound beside the stream,
The heaven and the earth could hardly survive,
They changed into
A fragrant and beautiful white peony Wuxiha [1],
Radiating brilliant light.
At sight of such a wonderful magical flower,
Nine-head devil Yeluli was so immersed in it
That he fondled it admiringly.
All devils were scrambling for the white flower,
When suddenly it changed into
Thousands of light arrows,
Shooting right into Yeluli's eyes.
In a sharp pain,
Yeluli rolled around with eyes closed,
Bellowed aloud,
And then escaped back to the caves underground,
Holding nine heads in his hands.

1 Peony Wuxiha: Manchu language, peony star.

Abukahehe was saved;
The heaven and the earth were rescued.
Abukahehe, Banmuhehe and Woleduohehe,
All together,
Expressed heartfelt thanks to Goddess Zhegulu.
Zhegulu,
Originally was Hedgehog Goddess in the heaven,
Who wore all over the light needles of souls,
Helped the three goddesses make all creatures,
And ensouled them.
The light on her,
Sharp in the extreme,
Was weaved of rays from the sun and the moon,
Could blind all creatures and devils,
And eclipse everything.

Since the disaster was all due to
Goddess Xisilin's oversleeping,
She was expelled out of the heaven and the earth,
And deprived of her goddess title
By the three goddesses.
Since then,
Xisilin changed her divine image,

And later became a male wild god under Yeluli,
Sowed his wild oats,
Galloped between the heaven and the earth,
Shook mountains and rocked the moon,
Did great harms to all creatures.

The custom that
Later generations
Liked to wear flowers in hair or topknot,
Was believed to intimidate and ward off the devils.
People all preferred white peonies when
Wearing flowers,
Arranging flowers,
Sticking paper-cut flowers,
And carving ice flowers.
The pure and white snowflakes,
Perfectly cut by Abukahehe,
Were also believed to
Ward off devils,
Purify the world,
And bless good luck
Generation after generation.

捌腓凌

世人为何宠爱白鹊、白鸟?

世人为何敬颂刺猬、地鼠的功劳?

千寿万寿的彩石呀,

是祖先的心爱之物,

朝夕难分难离。

石头是火,

石中有火,

是热火、力火、生命之火。

自从西斯林女神搬石御敌,

追打九头耶鲁里,

北方堆石成了山岳,

石山、石砬、石涧最多,

就是那时候留下来的。

石岩凝固成蛇脉,

石岩凝结成高山。

平川河谷就缺少了火石。

所以天下暴雪,

寒酷异常,

百兽百物藏洞求生。

阿布卡赫赫一心打败狠毒的

九头恶魔耶鲁里,

就要强壮筋骨。

突姆女神告诉阿布卡赫赫要多存石火，
吃石补身，
她便天天派侍女白腹号鸟、白脖厚嘴号鸟，
飞往东海采衔九纹石。
吃彩石就能壮力生骨，
吃彩石可以身长坚甲，
热照天地。
白腹号鸟、白脖厚嘴号鸟
勤快辛劳，
日夜不停，
衔回彩石累了，
归程时总要在
东天九叉神树上歇脚，
察望耶鲁里恶魔的动静。
千年松、万年桦，
开天时的古树是榆柳。
长叶柳树不仅能说人语、道人性，
而且能育人、运水、润虫蛙，
通天通地，称为天树。
天树通天桥，
通天桥路分九股，
九天九股住着宇宙神，
都是耶鲁里从地上赶上来的。
九股中每股分别住着三十个女神：

一九雷雪三十位，

二九溪涧三十位，

三九鱼鳖三十位，

四九天鸟长翼神，

五九地鸟短翼神，

六九水鸟肥脚神，

七九蛇猬迫日神，

八九百兽金洞神，

九九柳芍银花神，

统御寰天二百七，

三位赫赫位高尊。

征战恶魔需用兵器，

阿布卡赫赫命巴那姆赫赫出主意，

鸟生爪、

鱼生翅、

龟鳖生骨罩、

蛇脱皮草上飞、

百兽牙爪破坚石。

野猪最早无锋牙，

那是恶魔给安的。

耶鲁里的长角最无敌。

赫赫搓下身上的泥

做了无数米亚卡小神，

能伸能缩，

钻入地下，
钻进了耶鲁里的九头独角里。
耶鲁里头又痒又痛，
冲到天上，
独角让米亚卡神给钻了一半，
再不像过去那样又长又尖了。
耶鲁里的角掉在地上，
正巧赶上野猪拱地成沟，
要咬耶鲁里，
结果那个掉下的角
一下子扎在野猪的嘴上，
从此野猪长出了
又长又灵的獠牙，
比百兽都厉害。
耶鲁里头上滴的血
滴到了树林和岩石、土层里。
所以，
不少树木的木质
变成了红色，
有不少石头和土
也永远是红色的了。
耶鲁里疼得在天上打滚，
见到三百女神向它扑来，
便随着黑风逃到了

一条大河底下，

化成小小曲蛇[1]

藏进了泥水里。

三九天上的鱼母神，

见此情景追进水里，

变成一只机灵敏捷的小鲤鱼，

找到了耶鲁里，

从泥里咬住了耶鲁里

化形的小蚯蚓的尾巴，

蚯蚓身子一缩，掀起大浪泥沙，

搅混了清水，

鱼母神松口，

耶鲁里化为一阵恶风，又逃之夭夭。

西离女神[2]

因找到耶鲁里有功，

便成为宇宙中的鱼星辰——

鲤鱼星，

日夜还在天海边追寻着

恶魔耶鲁里。

从此，

世上的鲤鱼类

1 曲蛇：即蚯蚓。

2 西离女神：满族创世神话中的鱼母神。

总喜欢生活在深水水底，
以啃泥和水草根茎为食。

耶鲁里凭借西斯林的风威，
将光明吞进肚里，
天宇又变得黑漆无光。
恶风呼啸，
尘沙弥漫，
企图吹昏天上三百女神的头脑，
令其追踪不到它的身迹。
阿布卡赫赫便让一九云母神
变作一个永世计时星，
嘱她一定要永世侧身而行，
不要让耶鲁里认出来，
因为耶鲁里有西斯林的飓风，
刮起来云母神不能久停。
云母神便化作卧勒多赫赫
布星神属下的一位忠于职守的
塔其星神，
昼夜为众神计时，
再狂的恶风黑夜
也骗不了众神的眼睛。
可是耶鲁里总也抓不住她，
也认不出来她，

所以，耶鲁里永远不能
辨时辨方向，
总是不如阿布卡赫赫
畅行自如。

阿布卡赫赫又从身上搓落出泥，
生出兴克里女神，
能在黑暗里钻行，
迎接和引导太阳的光芒
照进暗夜，
这便是永世迎日的
鼠星神祗。
鼠星是迎日早临的女神。
离黎明时分还有若干时辰，
阿布卡赫赫担心黎明前黑暗里
耶鲁里仍偷袭捣乱，
就把身边的
三耳六眼灵兽派了出去，
永远地横卧在苍天之中，
头北尾南，
横跨中天，
总是极目远望高天，
寻找耶鲁里的踪影，
一直到太阳的光芒照彻寰宇，

星光隐灭，
辛勤而忠于职守的迎日灵兽
才从中天中消逝。
所以，
他是朝朝不知懒惰
爱日的神兽，
满语古语尊称他为
乌西哈布鲁古大神。
者固鲁女神总是
披着刺眼的光衫，
这是阿布卡赫赫赋予她的
万神神威。
万神的能耐和品德
都汇集到了她的身上，
能攻能守，
能进能退，
能隐能显，
能扩能缩，
能滚能行，
威勇无敌。
九头恶魔屡战屡败，
恼羞万分，
便找西斯林风魔神送去口信，
要一对一地比试高低。

双方都不要带帮手，
谁胜了谁就是
执掌寰天的额真达爷。
万物都要由他领辖，
由他创造，
由他衍生更替。

阿布卡赫赫便和卧勒多赫赫商议对策，
卧勒多女神对大姐说，
我虽不能去直接助阵，
但我可以暗中
帮助姐姐获胜。
我用布星的神工
将星群列成战阵，
连成一片，
当你征战累了时
可以在星辰上藏身歇脚，
我身上的银光长翅
可以为你打闪照路，
我能把星海堆成
山峦、沟谷、川壑，
阻挡耶鲁里的
逃遁，不让其施展淫威。
阿布卡赫赫听了十分高兴，

便与耶鲁里争杀在一起。
地动星移，
星撞星雷鸣电闪，
耶鲁里喷着黑风恶水，
天地昏黑，
石雨雷雹，
万物陨灭，
只有榆柳长寿齐天
延续至今。
百兽从此变得渺小，
藏匿于岩林沃雪之中。
硕兽巨鸟，
因畏惧西斯林的飓风，
传下瘦小敏捷的后代，
在林荫草莽中栖生。

耶鲁里被星光围困，
被光耀照晃，
被者固鲁女神的光衫刺射，
虽然与阿布卡赫赫
一对一地厮斗，
终神力难支，
便学阿布卡赫赫
站在星星上休息，

谁知耶鲁里想歇脚的星斗
并不是星体，
而是卧勒多赫赫很早就派去
查看双方厮打战情的
德登女神的头。
德登女神是阿布卡赫赫的一只脚，
身姿秀美修长，
与天地同长，
与天地同高，
性喜终日追逐风云，
无论多么高、
多么遥远的云天，
都可攀涉低于其肩，
可洞测寰宇的细微动息，
餐风啖星度日。
德登女神正在瞭看战况，
忽见九头恶魔耶鲁里仓惶降下，
便故意将自己的尖尖长发，
布散成一望无边的
空中星地，
骗住耶鲁里，
使他以为是一颗天星，
等耶鲁里双脚刚一踏上，
德登女神便将头身猛倾，

耶鲁里踩空，

头朝下一下子就堕落进了

德登女神脚踩着的地心里。

正巧，

地心正是巴那吉额姆[1]

身上的肚脐眼。

这里住着一位女神，

是巴那吉额姆

最宠爱的女儿福特锦力神。

她是生得四头六臂八足的大力神，

与德登女神同样是身高齐天，

只不过她不守视天穹，

而是护视九层天穹的下三层。

四头分视四方，

眼睛能观察到

鸟虫也飞不到的地方，

能看穿岩土峦岳。

她的六臂能够托天摇地，

拔山撼树，

能缚捉住千里之外的

飞鸟奔兔，

她闭眼伸手就能

采摘野果，

1　巴那吉额姆：即巴那姆赫赫，土地女神。

辨别百草，
她长着人脚、兽腿、鸟爪、百虫的足，
跑起来连风也追不到。
她的身姿与姊妹神
德登女神正相反，
粗矮雄阔，
像一座横亘千里的峰岩。
耶鲁里掉进其肚脐洞，
正被福特锦力神捉住，
她紧紧掐住耶鲁里的九头，
耶鲁里因有气光神功，
惊慌逃窜。
因为耶鲁里是化成光气跑走的，
在福特锦女神身上
从此留下许多气孔，
至今岩石中还常见到
像蜂窝似的洞穴，
就是当年耶鲁里
逃窜化气时留下来的。
耶鲁里逃跑后被放散的魔气，
化成了山冈恶瘴、世间疫病，
从此留到了世间，
贻害无穷。
耶鲁里被福特锦女神按住时，

抓下了片片黑色的骨甲，

变成了龟蛤蛛神，

爬进河谷和草间。

龟蛤蛛丝均可入卜，

因其本为耶鲁里的灵气残骨，

寓有灵气，

空际星阵为卧勒多赫赫聚星而成，

从此穹宇间日月相分，

不在一天，

相互追映。

空际有了天河星海，

白亮亮、光闪闪，

绵亘东西，

像一条顶天立地、

不可逾越的星山，

便是为拦截耶鲁里而筑成的。

Chapter VIII

Why are the white magpies and white birds worshiped in the world?
Why are the hedgehogs and squirrels praised in the world?
The eternal colorful stones,
Were the beloved of the ancestors,
That they could hardly live without,
Day and night.
The stone was fire,
Contained fire inside,
Which was the fire of heat,
The fire of power,
And the fire of life.
Since Goddess Xisilin moved stones to defend enemies,
And chased nine-head Yeluli,
The stones in the north heaped up into mountains,
Where many rocky hills, stones and ravines
Remained since then.
Stones solidified into snaky mountains,
And congealed into high peaks.
Thus the fire stones were insufficient
In plains and valleys.
As a result,
It snowed heavily all over the world;

Cold in the extreme,
All animals hid in caves for survival.
Abukahehe set her mind
To defeat the cruel nine-head Yeluli,
So she had to strengthen her bones and muscles.
Goddess Tumu told Abukahehe
To possess as many fire stones as possible,
And eat them to tone up her body.
Thus she sent her maids,
White-belly bird and white-neck thick-bill bird,
To carry nine-grain stones from the East Sea.
By eating the colorful stones
She could not only improve strength and promote bones,
But also grow solid armor all over the body,
Warming up the heaven and the earth.
White-belly bird and white-neck thick-bill bird,
Worked hard day and night.
When tired from carrying the colorful stones
On the journey back,
They usually stopped for a rest,
In the nine-branch trees of eastern heaven,
And watched Yeluli meanwhile.
One thousand years old as pines could be,
Ten thousand years old as birches could be,

The most ancient trees at the Time of Creation
Were elms and willows.
Long-leaf willows could
Not only speak human language and sense humanity,
But also cultivate people,
Carry water and nourish insects and frogs,
And connect the heaven and the earth,
Thus were called the Heaven Tree.
The Heaven Tree was the bridge to heaven,
Which divided into nine branches;
On the nine branches
Lived goddesses of the universe,
Who were driven there from the earth by Yeluli.
On each branch lived thirty goddesses:
On the first branch
Lived thirty goddesses of thunder and snow;
On the second branch
Lived thirty goddesses of rivers and streams;
On the third branch
Lived thirty goddesses of fish and turtles;
On the fourth branch
Lived thirty goddesses of long-wing heaven birds;
On the fifth branch
Lived thirty goddesses of short-wing earth birds;

On the sixth branch
Lived thirty goddesses of fat-palm water birds;
On the seventh branch
Lived thirty goddesses of snakes and hedgehogs;
On the eighth branch
Lived thirty goddesses of cave-living animals;
And on the ninth branch
Lived thirty goddesses of willows and peonies;
All of them,
Two hundred and seventy in total,
Were commanded by the three goddesses
Who held the highest position.
In view of the great need for weapons
In the war against the devils,
Abukahehe asked Banamuhehe
To propose some ideas.
Birds had claws,
Fish had fins,
Turtles had shells,
Snakes crawled like flying on the grass
After shedding their skin,
And beasts' teeth and paws could break solid rocks.
Wild boars originally had no sharp tusks,
But later were given a pair by the devil.

Abukahehe rubbed the soil off her body,
And made numerous little goddesses Yaka,
Who could extend and shrink at will.
Then, Yaka wormed into the ground,
And drilled into Yeluli's horn on his nine heads.
Feeling pain and itch,
Yeluli rushed into the sky,
With half of his horn drilled broken by goddesses Yaka,
Which was no longer long and sharp as before.
Just as Yeluli's half corn dropped down to the ground,
A wild boar happened to be there digging about,
Intending to bite Yeluli;
Coincidently,
The half horn stuck right onto the wild boar's snout.
From then on,
Wild boars wore a pair of long and useful tusks,
And were stronger than all animals.
From Yeluli's head dripped down the blood,
Dropping into the trees, rocks and the soil.
Therefore,
Many trees turned red,
And lots of rocks and soil
Became permanently red.
Rolling in pain in the sky,

Yet seeing three hundred goddesses coming at him,
Yeluli fled with the dark wind
To the bottom of a big river,
And changed into a little earthworm,
Hiding in the muddy river.
At sight of that,
The Fish Goddess on the third branch of heaven
Followed him into the river,
Changed into a clever and agile little carp,
Sought out Yeluli,
And bit the tail of the little earthworm
That changed from Yeluli in the mud.
The earthworm however shrank its body,
Stirred up muddy waves,
And roiled the clear water.
The Fish Goddess had to relax her bite,
Thus Yeluli slipped away,
Changing into a gust of evil wind.

Because of the merit in tracing Yeluli,
Goddess Xili[1] became
The Star of Fish in the universe,
The Carp Star,

1 Goddess Xili:The goddess of fish in creation myth of Manchu.

And still was chasing after the devil Yeluli,
In the sky and sea,
Day and night.
From then on,
All carps in the world
Tended to live at the bottom of deep water,
Eating soil and the waterweeds roots for food.

By virtue of Xisilin's severe wind strength,
Yeluli swallowed brightness,
Leaving the sky in utter darkness.
Evil wind roared,
Sand and dust pervaded,
With which Yeluli attempted to
Blow the three hundred heaven goddesses dizzy,
So that they could not trace him any more.
Abukahehe asked the Cloud Goddess on the first branch
To change into an eternal-timer star,
And enjoined her to keep sidling forever,
So as not to be recognized by Yeluli.
Since Yeluli took advantage of Xisilin's severe wind,
Cloud Goddess was unable to stay long;
She thus turned into
The dedicated Star Goddess Taqi,

Who was subordinate to Star Goddess Woleduohehe,
And in charge of time keeping for goddesses day and night,
So even the evil wind and dark night
Could not fool the goddesses' eyes at all.
However,
Yeluli could never catch up with her,
Nor could he recognize or trace her;
Therefore,
Yeluli could never identify time and directions,
Nor could he match Abukahehe in free moving.

Abukahehe rubbed mud again off her body,
And created Goddess Xingkeli,
Who could fly in the dark,
Greet and lead the sunlight into the dark night;
Held up as Mouse Star Goddess,
He greeted the sun for life.
Mouse Star was the goddess
Who greeted the sun in the early morning.
But there were still several hours before daybreak.
Worrying that
Yeluli might send a sneak attack
Or create some disturbance
In the dark before daybreak,

Abukahehe sent her three-ear six-eye spirit beast,
To lie in the sky always and forever;
Head facing to the north,
Tail orienting toward the south,
The beast stretched across the central sky,
And looked into the sky as far as it could,
Seeking for Yeluli's trace all the time;
Not until the sunlight shone throughout the world,
And the starlight dimmed and disappeared,
Would the dedicated sun-greeting spirit beast
Fade away from the central sky.
Therefore,
As a tireless sun-adoring spirit beast in the morning,
He was hailed in ancient Manchu language as
God Wuxihabulugu.
Goddess Zhegulu always wore glaring light garment,
And possessed the magical power of all gods
Bestowed by Abukahehe.
Abilities and moralities of all gods
Assembled in her:
Offending and defending,
Advancing and retiring,
Appearing and disappearing,
Expanding and contracting,

Rolling and moving,
Unrivaled in bravery.
Failing the battles one after another,
Flying into a rage out of shame,
The nine-head devil
Asked wind devil Xisilin to send Abukahehe a message,
Requiring a one-to-one game.
Both sides were not allowed to seek for help,
And the one who won
Would be the world-dominating Ezhendaye.
All creatures would be in the charge of him,
Created by him,
And live or die at his diposal.

Abukahehe conferred with Woleduohehe for advice;
Woleduohehe said to her elder sister,
"Though I could not root for you openly in the battle,
I could secretly help you to win for sure.
With my magical power of star disposal,
I could lay out stars into strategic arrays,
And connect them together,
On which you could hide for a rest,
When you are tired from the battle;
With the silver-light wings on me,

I could flash lightning

To illuminate the way for you;

I could heaped the stars into

Mountains, valleys, rivers and gullies,

Which could hinder Yeluli

From escaping or using his evil magic."

Hearing that,

Abukahehe was overjoyed,

Thus fought against Yeluli.

Earth quaked,

Stars moved and collided,

Lightning flashed

And thunder rumbled;

Yeluli blew out dark wind and evil water,

Leaving the heaven and the earth in the dark.

Rocks fell,

Rain poured,

Thunder rumbled,

And hail dropped.

All creatures died out,

Except the elms and the willows

That could live as long as the heaven,

And remain alive up to now.

Since then,

All animals became small,
Hiding in the snow, rocks and forests.
Scared of Xisilin's severe wind,
Huge beasts and large birds,
Delivered small but agile offspring,
Who could survive in the wood or grassland.

Besieged by starlight,
Bewildered by brilliant rays,
Pierced by Goddess Zhegulu's light garment,
Though struggling to
Fight against Abukehehe one to one,
Yeluli finally became exausted in the extreme,
And followed Abukahehe
To stop on a star for rest;
Out of his expectation,
The star on which Yeluli wanted to take a rest
Was not a star at all,
But the head of Goddess Dedeng,
Who was sent by Woleduohehe
To check the progress of the battle.
As Abukahehe's one foot,
Goddess Dedeng was slender and beautiful.
Long as the length of heaven and earth,

High as the height between heaven and earth,
She was keen on
Chasing after wind and cloud all day long;
No matter how high and far the cloud was,
She would climb up to it,
Leaving everything below her shoulders;
Apart from that,
She could observe subtle changes in the world,
Drink wind and eat stars for life.
Goddess Dedeng was watching the battle progress.
When she suddenly saw
The nine-head devil Yeluli descending in panic,
She deliberately stretched her sharp hair
Into a vast star land in the heaven,
Which fooled Yeluli into thinking it a star.
As soon as Yeluli stepped on it,
Goddess Dedeng abruptly tilted her head and body,
So that Yeluli lost his footing,
Falling with head over heels,
Right down into the earth center,
Where Goddess Dedeng stood on.
Coincidently,
The earth center was Banajiemu [1]'s belly button,

1 Banaji'emu: Namely Banamuhehe, the goddess of the earth.

Where lived a goddess,
Who was Banajiemu's favorite daughter,
Strength Goddess Futejin.
A goddess of great strength,
With four heads, six arms and eight feet,
She was as tall as Goddess Dedeng;
Yet she didn't guard the heaven,
But watched on the lower three layers
Of the nine-layer heaven.
With her four heads
She could watch four directions;
With her eyes open,
She could observe somewhere
That even the birds and insects could not fly to,
And see through the rocks and mountains;
With her six arms,
She could raise the sky and rock the earth,
Move the mountains and shake the trees,
And capture flying birds and running rabbits miles away;
With her hands stretched out and eyes closed,
She could pick the wild fruits,
And identify all kinds of grasses.
Possessed of human feet, beast legs,
Bird claws and insect feet,

She could run so fast
That even the wind could not catch up.
Unlike her sister Goddess Dedeng,
Her figure was thick and broad,
Like a rocky mountain,
Stretching miles away.
Yeluli fell into her belly-button cave,
And was caught by Strength Goddess Futejin,
Who tightly gripped Yeluli's nine heads;
But with his air-and-light magic,
Yeluli fled away in panic.
Because he escaped by changing into air and light,
He left on Goddess Futejin's body
Numerous air holes since then;
Now the common honeycomb-like holes in the rocks,
Formed when Yeluli Fled and changed into air.
After Yeluli fled away,
The diffused evil air changed into
Evil miasma around mountains,
And epidemic disease among creatures,
Leaving endless trouble to the world since then.
The pieces of his black carapaces
Grabbed and torn down By Goddess Fudejin,
Turned separately into

The gods of turtle, clam and spider,
And crawled into the rivers and grasses.
Since then,
Turtles, clams and spider silk,
Were all used for divination,
Because they were originally
Yeluli's anima and debris,
And possessed his aura.
Star arrays in the sky
Were disposed by Wodeduohehe;
So from then on,
The sun and the moon in the heaven separated,
Never meeting in the sky,
But chasing after each other.
In the sky emerged
The Heaven River and the Star Sea,
White and shiny,
Stretching from east to west,
Which were built to intercept Yeluli,
Like an unbridgeable star mountain,
Standing between the heaven and the earth.

玖腓凌

天上的杀戮是怎么平息的？
世上的生灵是如何传世的？
耶鲁里恶魔被福特锦力神缚捉，
掐破肤甲，
轧露光气，
耶鲁里从此恶风骤减，
九个头上有四个头的眼睛
只能洞测黑夜，
惧慑太阳火光。
但是，
恶念凶欲不死，
企望挟天为主，
便于日月降落后的黑夜里，
悄悄冲向青空，
口喷黑风恶水，
淹没了穹宇大地。
阿布卡赫赫刚升到天上，
便得到德登女神的报告，
可耶鲁里已经
将兴恶里鼠星女神捉住，
放走了神鹰，
并把迎面冲来的阿布卡赫赫身上的

九座石山、九片柳林、
九条溪流、九只兽骨
编成的战裙扯了下来。
这是阿布卡赫赫的护身战裙。
阿布卡赫赫丢掉了护身战裙，
只好逃了出来，
在众星神的保护下，
逃回九层天上，
疲惫不堪，
昏倒在滚动着金光的太阳河旁。
太阳河边有一棵高大的神树，
神树上住着一位名叫
昆哲勒的九彩神鸟。
它扯下自己身上的羽毛，
为阿布卡赫赫
擦着腰脊上的伤口，
用九彩神光编制护腰战裙，
又衔来金色的太阳河水，
给阿布卡赫赫冲洗着伤口，
使阿布卡赫赫很快伤愈如初。
阿布卡赫赫身穿九彩神羽战裙，
从太阳河水中
慢慢苏醒过来。
巴那姆赫赫将自己身上生息的

虎、豹、熊、鹿、蟒、蛇、
狼、野猪、蜥蜴、鹰、雕、
江海鱼虾、百虫等魂魄摄来，
让每一个兽禽神魂
献出一招神技，
帮助阿布卡赫赫。
又从自己身上献出一块魂骨，
由昆哲勒神鸟在太阳河边，
用彩羽重新又为阿布卡赫赫
编织了护腰战裙。
从此，
天才真正变成了
现在这个颜色，
阿布卡赫赫也真正有了
无敌于寰宇的神威。

姊妹三人在众禽兽的辅佐之下，
打败了九头恶魔耶鲁里，
使它变成了一个
只会在夜间怪嚎的九头恶鸟，
埋在巴那姆赫赫身下的最底层，
不能再扰害天穹。
可是，
巴那姆赫赫身边还生活着许多

喜欢穿穴而居的生命，
如蝼蚁、穿山甲、地鼠等，
耶鲁里的败魂还时常出世脱化
满尼、满盖，
践害人世。
然而，
由于阿布卡赫赫打败耶鲁里时，
将它九个头上
五个头的双眼取下，
使它变成了瞎子，
最怕光明和篝火，
只要燃放篝火，
点取冰灯，
照亮暗隅，
九头鸟便不敢危害世间了。
从此，
才在世间留下夜点冰灯、
拜祭篝火的古习。
阿布卡赫赫从此才成为一位
永远不死、不可战胜的穹宇母神，
维佑天地，
传袭百世。

阿布卡赫赫

又派神鹰哺育了一女婴，
使她成为世上第一位大萨满，
神鹰哺育用的奶水，
便是昆哲勒从太阳河衔来的
生命与智慧的神夔。
空际的大鹰星本、是由卧勒多赫赫
用绳索系住左脚，
命它协佐德登女神守护天穹的。
因为耶鲁里扯断了鹰的神索，
鹰星在天空中变幻得最大，
其星羽突闪突现。
阿布卡赫赫便命她哺育了
世上第一个通晓神界、兽界、
灵界、魂界的
智者——大萨满。
神鹰受命后，
便用昆哲勒神鸟
衔来太阳河中
生命与智慧的神夔
喂育萨满，
用卧勒多赫赫的神光
启迪萨满，
使她通晓星卜天时；
用巴那姆赫赫的肤肉

丰润萨满，
使她运筹神技；
用耶鲁里自生自育的奇功
诱导萨满，
使她有传播男女媾育的医术。
女大萨满才成为世间
百聪百伶、百慧百巧的万能神者，
抚安世界，
传替百代。

天荒地老，
星云更世，
不知又过了多少亿万年，
北天冰海南流，
洪涛冰山盖野。
地上是水，
天上也是水，
大地上只有代敏大鹰
和一个女人留世，
生下了人类。
这便是洪涛后的女大萨满，
成为人类始母神，
是阿布卡赫赫把太阳河昆哲勒神
派到水中，

从此冰水才有了温暖，
才生育出水虫、水草，
重新有鱼虾、水蛇、
水獭、水狸，
又在东海有了人身鱼神，
受太阳之光，
不少水虫变为人首鱼身的
河湖沼海之神，
因是受阳光而育，
应阳光而生，
故常罩七彩光衫，
称为德立格女神。
为使世间能分辨方向，
阿布卡赫赫让自己身边的
五个方向女神下来，
给人类指点方向。
西方洼勒格女神
一步三蹦地先走到了人世，
随后到的是：
东方德立格女神和
北方阿玛勒格女神以及
南方朱勒格女神，
中位为都伦巴女神，
由五位女神职掌方位。

对于大地上的残留汪洋，
阿布卡赫赫拔下身上的腋毛，
令其化成了无数条水龙——木克木都力，
朝朝暮暮地吞水。
从此，
又在大地上出现了无数条
又粗又宽、又长又弯的
道口江河和沟岔，
有像毕拉一样的河，
像乌拉一样的江，
像岔儿汉一样的小支流，
养育着阿布卡赫赫的子孙——人类。

不知又经过多少万年，
洪荒远古，
阿布卡赫赫人称
阿布卡恩都力大神，
高卧九层云天之上，
呵气为霞，
喷火为星，
山河宁静，
阿布卡恩都力也学
巴那姆赫赫一样懒散慢惰，
性喜酣睡。

所以，

北地朔野寒天，

冰河覆地，

雪海无垠，

万物不生。

巴那姆额姆教人穴居地下，

筑室洞窟，

故北人大都深室九梯，

刺猬、蝙蝠均为安全守神。

耶鲁里常潜出施毒烟害人，

疮疖、天花灭室穴生命。

雅格哈女神天性擅视百草，

索活[1]、它卡[2]、佛库它拉[3]、

省折[4]、山茶[5]为人所食，

百花为人送香气，

百树为人衣其皮，

百兽为人食其肉，

熏香为人祛疮除秽

敬祖神。

阿布卡恩都力送给人间

1 索活：满语，意为甜酱菜。
2 它卡：满语，意为野芥菜
3 佛库它拉：满语，意为蕨菜。
4 省哲：满语，意为蘑菇。
5 山茶：满语，意为木耳。

瞒尼神九十二位，

其中有：战神、箭神、石神、

痘神、瘸神、头疼神、

噬血神、大力神、狩猎神、

穴居神、飞涧神、舟筏神、

育婴神、产孕神、媾交神、

断事神、卜算神、驭火神、

唤水神、山雪神、乌春[1]神、

玛克辛[2]神、说古神，等等。

重要的瞒爷神，

向子嗣传播古史故事。

最古，

先人用火是拖亚拉哈大神所赐；

阿布卡恩都力未给人以火之前，

人们茹血生食，

常室于地下，

同蝼鼠无异。

雪消出洞，

落雪入地，

人蛇同穴，

人蝠同眠，

十有一生。

1 乌春：满语，意为歌。

2 玛克辛：满语，意为舞。

阿布卡恩都力
额上突生红瘤“其其旦”，
化为美女，
脚踏火烧云，
身披红霞星光衫，
嫁与雷神西思林为妻。
雷神西思林也同
风神西斯林一样，
原来同是
阿布卡恩都力的爱子，
雷神西思林，
是阿布卡恩都力的
酣声化形而成的巨神，
火发、白身、长手，
喜驰游寰宇，
声啸裂地劈天，
勇不可挡；
而风神西斯林早生于
西思林雷神，
是阿布卡恩都力的
两双巨脚所化生，
风驰电掣，
不负于雷神的肆虐，
乘其外游盗走其其旦女神，

欲与女神媾孕子孙，
播送大地，
使人类得以绵续。
可是其其旦女神见大地
冰厚齐天，
无法育子，
便私盗阿布卡恩都力的
心中神火临凡。
怕神火熄灭，
她便把神火吞进肚里，
嫌两脚行走太慢，
便以手为足助驰。
天长日久，
她终于在运火过程中，
被神火烧成虎目、虎耳、
豹头、豹须、獾身、鹰爪、
猞猁尾的一只怪兽，
变成拖亚拉哈大神。
她四爪踏火云，
巨口喷烈焰，
驱冰雪，
逐寒霜，
驰如电闪，
光照群山，

为大地和人类送来了火种，
招来了春天。
天上所以要打雷，
就是禀赋暴烈的雷神弟弟
向风神哥哥在索要爱妻呢！

Chapter IX

How were the battles and killings in the heaven settled down?
How were lives in the world passed on?
When Yeluli was captured by Strength Goddess Futejin,
His carapace was pinched broken,
His essence air and light leaked out,
So the evil wind blown by Yeluli weakened abruptly,
And only eyes on four of his nine heads
Could perceive the dark night,
But feared to look into the glaring light or fire.
However,
He never quit his evil intentions and violent desire;
In an attempt to
Control the heaven and command all goddesses,
In the darkness between sunset and moonrise,
He secretly rushed into the sky,
Blew black wind and evil water,
Which flooded the heaven and the earth.
Not until Abukahehe flew up to the heaven
To get the news from Goddess Dedeng,
Had Yeluli caught Mouse Star Goddess Xing'eli,
Released the divine eagle,
And ripped off Abukahehe's costume,

Which was weaved of

Nine rocky mountains, nine willow forests,

Nine rivers and nine animal bones.

That was Abukahehe's armed costume;

Without it,

Abukahehe had to fled,

Under the protection of the star goddesses,

Back to the ninth layer of the heaven,

And fainted at the glaring Sun River,

Exhausted to death.

At the side of the Sun River

Was a tall sacred tree;

And on the sacred tree

Lived a nine-color divine bird Kunzhele,

Who pulled off her own feather

To clean the wound on Abukahehe's spine,

Weaved a waist-protecting costume

With the nine-color sacred light,

And fetched water from the golden Sun River,

To wash wound for Abukahehe,

So she could rapidly restore.

Wearing nine-color armed costume,

Abukahehe slowly came around at the Sun River.

Banamuhehe took the souls from

Tiger, leopard, bear, deer, python, snake,
Wolf, boar, lizard, hawk, eagle,
Fish and shrimp in river and sea, and insects,
Who all lived on her body,
And ask each of them to present one magical skill
To help Abukahehe;
Then she donated one spiritual bone of her own,
With which the divine bird Kunzhele at the side of Sun River
Weaved her colorful feather
Into a girdle costume for Abukahehe.
From then on,
The sky really turned into the color as it is today,
And Abukahehe truly possessed
The magical power unrivaled in the world.

Under the assistance of all mythical birds and animals,
Three sister goddesses defeated nine-head devil Yeluli,
Changed him into a nine-head evil bird howling at night,
And buried him at the lowest layer under Banamuhehe,
So he could never make disturbance in the heaven.
However,
By the side of Banamuhehe
Lived many cave dwellers,
Like mole crickets, ants, pangolins, diglett, etc;

Thus Yeluli's defeated soul
Frequently came into the world,
Transformed into Manni or Mangai,
And became a harm to the world.
Fortunately,
When Abukahehe defeated Yeluli,
She took the eyes off the five heads of nine,
Making him blind,
Who was scared of brightness and campfire;
So long as people set off campfire,
Or lit ice lantern to illuminate the darkness,
The nine-head bird would dare not to do evil.
Since then,
The ancient custom of lighting ice lantern
And worshiping campfire at night,
Had been Passed down in the world.
Abukahehe consequently became
An immortal and invincible heaven goddess,
Protecting and blessing the heaven and the earth,
Passing on oracles from generation to generation.

Abukahehe
Sent the sacred eagle to feed a baby girl,
And raised her up into the first Shaman in the world.

The milk fed by the sacred eagle,
Was the sacred nourishment of life and intelligence,
Carried from the Sun River by Kunzhele.
The Eagle Star in the sky,
Whose left foot was originally tied
With a rope by Woleduohehe,
Was ordered to assist Goddess Dedeng
In guarding the heaven.
Since Yeluli broke the rope on sacred eagle's foot,
Eagle Star could change infinitely in the sky,
With its starry feather flickering and glimmering.
Abukahehe then ordered her to feed
The Chief Shaman,
A sage who was the first to perceive
The divine world,
The animal world,
The spirit world,
And the soul world.
Receiving the order,
The sacred eagle fed Shaman
With the sacred soup of life and intelligence,
Which was fetched by sacred bird Kunzhele,
From the Sun River;
Enlightened Shaman

With the sacred light of Woleduohehe,
Giving her insight into astromancy;
Plumped and smoothened Shaman
With the flesh and skin of Banamuhehe,
Enabling her to cast spells;
Guided Shaman
With Yeluli's magical power of self-fertility,
Teaching her to spread the medical skill of fertility
Between men and women.
Consequently,
The female Shaman became a wise and quick-witted,
Intelligent, skillful and omnipotent oracle,
Who guarded and stabilized the world,
Inherited the title and passed down the tradition,
For hundreds of generations.

The heaven and the sun aged,
The stars and clouds altered;
Before one knew how many billions of years had passed,
The ice sea in northern heaven flowed southward,
And riptide and iceberg flooded the field.
The earth was covered with water,
And so was the heaven;
On the earth only survived Sacred Eagle Daimin

And a woman,
Who gave birth to human beings.
She was the female Chief Shaman
Who survived the flood,
And became the ancient mother goddess of mankind;
Only when Abukahehe
Sent the sun and Goddess Kunzhele to the water,
would the icy water begin to warm up,
In which
Water bugs and waterweeds grew,
Fish, shrimps, water snakes,
Otters and beavers reappeared in turn.
Then in the eastern sea,
Emerged a human-shaped fish goddess;
By virtue of the brilliant sunlight,
Many water bugs turned into
Human-head and fish-body goddesses
Of river, lake, pond and sea.
Fertilized by sunlight,
Born in sun,
The human-shaped fish goddess
Usually wore a seven-color sunlight costume,
Thus was known as Goddess Delige.
To enable people to distinguish directions in the world,

Abukahehe sent to the earth
The five goddesses of directions,
Who could give people directions.
Skipping and hopping,
The West Goddess Walege,
Was the first to arrive on the earth;
Then Closely followed by:
East Goddess Delige,
North Goddess Amalege,
South Goddess Zhulege,
And Center Goddess Dulunba,
Who were in charge of directions together.
To cope with the residual ocean on the earth,
Abukahehe plucked out her armpit hairs,
And changed them into numerous water dragons,
Mukemuduli,
Who kept swallowing water day and night.
From then on,
On the earth emerged numerous
Thick, broad, long and crooked rivers and gullies,
Some were small rivers like Bila,
Some were big rivers like Wula,
Some were little tributary like Chaerhan,
All Fostered Abukahehe's offspring——Mankind.

Then several millions of years passed;
In the remote antiquity,
Abukahehe was honored as God Abuka'enduli,
Lying high over the nine-layer sky,
Blowing air into rosy clouds,
Spitting fire into stars,
Maintaining peace and stability in the world.
As sluggish as Banamuhehe,
Abuka'enduli tended to sleep all day long.
As a consequence,
In the north of the world,
The fields grew wild,
The climate got cold,
The icy rivers covered the land,
The snowy sea stretched without end,
And all creatures died out.
Banamu'emu taught humans to
Live in caves underground,
And construct rooms in caves;
So most northern people lived in caves
Deep underground with nine stairs,
And worshiped hedgehogs and bats as patron saints.
Yeluli often sneaked out

To poison humans with toxic smoke,
Thus sores and smallpox killed cave-living lives.
Goddess Yageha by nature
Was good at identifying grasses,
So Suohuo [1],Taka [2], Fukutala [3],
Shengzhe [4], and Shancha [5]
Served as food for humans;
Flowers brought fragrance to humans,
Trees supplied barks as clothing to humans,
Animals sacrificed their meet as food for people,
Incense was burned to dispel sores and filth
And to worship ancestral gods.

Abuka'enduli sent the world ninety-two Manni gods,
Including:
War God, Arrow God, Rock God,
Blain God, Cripple God, Headache God,
Bloodsucking God, Strength God, Hunting God,
Cave-living God, Ravine God, Raft God,
Infant-care God, Pregnancy-and-delivery God, Copulation God,
Decision-making God, Augury God, Fire-control God,

1 Suohuo: Manchu language, sweet vegetable.
2 Taka: Manchu language, wild mustard.
3 Fukutala: Manchu language, fern.
4 Shengzhe: Manchu language, mushroom.
5 Shancha: Manchu language, agaric.

Rain God, Mountain-snow God, Wuchun[1] God,

Makexin[2] God, Story-telling God and so on.

The high-status Manye God,

Spread the story of ancient history and heritage.

At ancient time,

The fire used by ancestors

Was given by goddess Tuoyalaha;

Before Abuka'enduli gave fire to humans,

People drank blood and ate raw meat,

And lived underground just as crickets and rats did.

They came out of caves when snow melted,

Went underground when snow fell;

Shared caves with snakes,

Slept together with bats;

Thus only one out of ten people could survive.

On Abuka'enduli's forehead

Abruptly grew out a red tumor Qiqidan,

Who changed into a beauty

In rosy-cloud, star-light garment,

And married Thunder God Xicilin.

Like Wind God Xisilin,

Thunder God Xicilin originally was

---

1 Wuchun: Manchu language, song.

2 Makexin: Manchu language, dance.

The beloved son of Abuka'enduli.

Thunder God Xicilin

Was a giant god who

Changed from Abuka'enduli's sound of snoring,

Possessed fire hair, white skin and long hands,

galloped around the world at will,

Roared aloud so as to crack the earth and split the sky,

Thus was unrivaled in bravery.

Wind God Xisilin was born before Thunder God Xicilin;

Changed from Abuka'enduli's two huge feet,

He flew swiftly like wind and lightning,

And was not second to Thunder God in strength.

While Thunder God travelled outside,

Wind God stole Goddess Qiqidan,

In an attempt to copulate and breed offspring with her,

Spread their offspring to the earth,

So that humans could live long and prosper.

But Goddess Qiqidan saw

The ice on the earth was so thick as to reach the sky,

Where it's unsuitable to breed offspring;

So she secretly stole

The sacred fire from Abukahehe's heart,

And took it to the earth.

For fear that the sacred fire might extinguished,

She swallowed it into stomach;
Thinking it too slow to walk on two feet,
She used hands as feet for running.
Carrying the sacred fire for a long time,
She finally was burnt into a monster,
With tiger's eyes and ears,
Leopard's head and whiskers,
Badger's body,
Eagle's claws and lynx's tail,
And became Goddess Tuoyalaha,
Who stood on fire clouds with four claws,
Spit roaring flame from huge mouth,
Dispelled ice and snow,
Drove off cold frost,
Ran swiftly like lightning,
Illuminated the mountains,
Carried fire and brought spring
To the earth and mankind.
The reason why it thundered in the sky was that,
The hot-tempered Thunder God
Was claiming for his beloved wife,
From his elder brother Wind God!